D0969927

A Boundary Waters Fishing Guide

by Michael Furtman

*Illustrated
by Alan Linné*

NORTHWORD PRESS, INC.
Minocqua

A Boundary Waters Fishing Guide. Copyright 1984 ©, 1990 © & 1994 © by Michael J. Furtman. All rights reserved. Printed in the United States of America. No part of this book may be used, reproduced or transmitted in any form or by any means, including photocopying, recording or by any information storage and retrieval system without written permission except in the case of brief quotations embodied in critical articles or reviews.

Library of Congress Catalog Card Number: 84-70248

Published by **NorthWord Press, Inc.**
P.O. Box 1360
Minocqua, WI 54548

Cover Photo by Lynn Rogers
Interior photos by author except as noted

ISBN: 1-55971-073-X Paperback

Acknowledgments

I did not generate most of this information. Much of the credit must go to those who travelled this land before me, such as my father, and passed on their knowledge. I must thank those contemporaries who shared their knowledge with me in preparation for this book and those professionals in the Minnesota Department of Natural Resources, Ontario Ministry of Natural Resources, and those in the U.S. Forest Service. Without the field work of these souls who care for our natural world and their cooperation in allowing me to ransack their files, this work could not have been completed.

I must also thank Mary Jo Furtman who assisted me in my research, lent me her support and belief in the project, and patiently shared our time with this work.

Dedication

This volume is dedicated to my father, Ralph Furtman, whose patience and love of nature instilled in his children a deep respect for the out-of-doors; and to my late mother Bernice Furtman, whose vacations were not to glamorous cities or resorts but to the northwoods where her own love and understanding nurtured us in our wild adventures; and to my wife, Mary Jo, who has become my severest critic and greatest supporter in my writing and my first choice of partners to share my trips into the wild; and to my friends who encouraged me through the years to write.

Table of Contents

The Canoe Country's remote lakes contain some big fish. This nice northern fell for a fly.

Chapter 1

Goin' Up North

LARGE ENOUGH to feed one's imagination, the Boundary Waters Canoe Area Wilderness (BWCAW) and Quetico Provincial Park area are a haven for thousands of canoeists. They are also a haven for lots of fish. With over 2 million acres of woods and water and a border that extends for almost one hundred and fifty miles, the Quetico and Boundary Waters provides nearly unbounded opportunities for personal exploration. If one of your passions is fishing, the area is doubly blessed. Festooned with garlands of sparkling lakes, nearly each and every one containing fish, the Canoe Country can conjure up daydreams of large fish amongst even the least imaginative.

The first time I put foot and paddle into the Boundary Waters it was not known as such. At the time the American side's official monicker was the Superior Roadless Area, just a backwoods parcel of the Superior National Forest. We simply called it goin' up north. Or, if in the mood to be a little more specific, we said we were going "close by Ely" or "up the

Gunflint Trail." These references may date me. Perhaps by too much because I'm not that old. It's just that my family frequented the area often and my father, not one to let a bunch of kids cut down too much on his fishing, brought us along to feed the bugs. I was around five years old on the first trip that I can remember.

Our purpose in going "up north" was not just to canoe and camp. These were means to an end. The real reason we went there was to fish.

It was a long standing family tradition, dating back to the late 1940's, to make an early season lake trout trip. In those days the lake trout season opened earlier than it does now in order to take better advantage of the superb lake trout fishing to be had after the ice-out. At times we fished areas of a lake that had lost their ice only a matter of hours or days before our arrival, the rest of the lake sometimes still covered with the blue-black of rotting ice. Snow at night was not unusual and it was a fairly simple matter to find snow hidden in the shadows.

During those years, before the Boundary Waters was declared a wilderness area by law and motors were still being used throughout its length and breadth, fishermen were by far the most common group of visitors. While I suspect they enjoyed the scenery and pleasures of camping in this beautiful and rugged country no less than today's canoeing public, the main purpose of their trip was to fish. They came from all parts of this country to sample what truly was, and still is, some of the finest fishing anywhere.

Most of these people were experienced fishermen and those that were not hired one of the many fishing guides that made their livelihood in this land of woods and water. Because they were coming to fish first and camp second, they were well prepared with the tackle and knowledge needed to take their catch. And because they had motors to do the

My father, center, and two friends on an early season lake trout trip. Tuscarora Lake, May, 1950.

work, they could lug along a few extra pounds of fishing gear, not to mention the extra ease of fishing from a motor powered canoe. Little time was wasted on waters they knew nothing about.

Today, things are different. With the declaration of a wilderness status for the Boundary Waters and the near elimination of the use of outboard motors in the BWCAW and Quetico, more and more of the area's visitors are there to enjoy the special solitude and remoteness. You could watch the change in the user groups as each phase of the restrictions on motor routes was implemented. More and more the people came to canoe and camp first and fishing became a secondary concern.

This is as it should be. While the Canoe Country's fishing is undeniably a big attraction, it is the magic of wilderness that comprises the region's true value. One may find fishing in many places; the tonic of expansive solitude is a much rarer commodity.

Still, to someone who had fished this area for years it came as quite a shock to find people up there who couldn't give a hoot about fishing. Equally as confusing was seeing folks who had fishing equipment with them but had assembled such a poor array as to be virtually worthless.

Once, after completing the portage into a favorite lake trout lake, we strung up our rods and decided to do a little trolling on our way to select a campsite. We were lucky enough to pick up a half dozen lakers as we paddled along but, when we rounded the bend near the campsite of our choice, we found it occupied. Disheartened, we turned the canoe down the lake. As we began to get turned around, we latched on to a dandy lake trout. All activity ceased except for the fight and a more than usual interest by the group watching us from the campsite we had hoped to use. When the fish began to tire, and we eased it up to the canoe, one of the camp's occupants apparently could stand it no longer. He slid his canoe into the lake and paddled furiously out to us. As he neared, he called out, "What didja catch?"

"A nice laker," I replied, "it's the seventh one today."

"Geez," he returned chagrinned, "we've been fishin' this lake for six days for walleyes and haven't caught a one, let alone a lake trout."

Now I don't like to play one-upmanship, but I thought maybe he would like to know. "It doesn't surprise me that you haven't caught any walleyes, there aren't any in this lake, nor within four portages. It is a good lake trout lake though."

He never said a word. Turning his canoe around he paddled back to his camp shaking his head. I don't know if he caught any lakers after that. I hope he did.

You don't have to be that confused to not catch fish. Many of the individuals that canoe this area hope to catch a few fish along the way and may have a fair idea of what kind of fish to expect on their route. But fishing in Lake Minnesewer back home is often much different than fishing up north. Sitting at home and planning a trip to this area can conjure up dreams of big fish and fresh filleted shore lunches. Knowing what to do and what to use once you get there, well that can be quite different than what you had foreseen.

On a more recent trip, one that I thought I had carefully researched, we were nearly flummoxed. We were to be out for six days, alternately camping then moving on each day. I knew that we wanted to camp on lakes X, Y and Z so I dutifully found out as much as I could about the fishing in each of those lakes. I was not too concerned about the lakes we planned merely to cross. You know what they say about the best laid plans of mice and men.

Nearing the end of the trip we were caught in a terrible thunder and lightning storm. We quickly made for shore, and as the storm seemed to be a large one with no end in sight, we madly set up camp. It blew and rained the rest of the day with the miserable precipitation finally letting up about supper time. Grateful for the chance to make a quick dinner, we piled out of the tents and grabbed the food bag. Somehow, in the confusion of the cloudburst, the stuffsack containing the food had not been put under shelter. The only things salvageable were some spaghetti noodles and the peanut butter. My wife threatened to make a peanut butter sauce to go with the spaghetti. I decided to go fishing.

The wind was still whistling fiercely down the length of the lake, whitecaps building to near three feet as they approached our campsite on the point. Desperate for an edible dinner, I tried fishing from shore. Three things quickly became evident.

The wind was too strong to cast into on the windward side of the point and the water too shallow on the lee side. The third thing was that, since we had not planned on fishing this lake, let alone camp on it, I did not bother to find out what was in it. Dejectedly, I walked back to camp. My wife was beginning to make the peanut butter sauce for the noodles.

To make a long story short, if that is still possible, I decided it was calm enough on the lee side of the point to slide the canoe out into a little deeper water. With one man handling the canoe while the other fished, it was barely possible to keep from capsizing. Now all I had to do was figure out how to catch whatever might be in this lake.

The lakes surrounding this one had either lake trout or smallmouth bass in them. A few had both. I decided it looked more like a smallmouth lake than a trout lake and made my tackle selection. I tried a top water plug. Nothing. I put on a shallow running plug. Zilch. I tried on a jig. Zero. Spoons and spinners produced the same results. I went to live bait and tried a leech and floating jig combination. No strikes. Finally I put on a small bait hook and a plain leech.

The area we could fish, because of the strong wind, was small. It looked good and because it was the only spot we could fish and I wasn't optimistic about the palatability of the concoction simmering in camp, I fished it thoroughly with each new selection from the tackle box.

On the very next cast I felt a tremendous strike. Perhaps it was that I really didn't expect to catch anything at this point, but I missed on the set. Rebaiting the hook, I tossed it into the same spot, this time to hook the fish. When I set the hook, a green slab leapt skyward. A bass! So I was right, I thought, there are smallmouth in this lake. It wasn't until I boated the fish that I realized my mistake.

Friends, there is only one thing scarcer than a honest politician and that's a largemouth bass in the Boundary Waters.

But that is what this fish was, and so was the next.

Though I was surprised by their presence, I was grateful for it. With a couple of three pound bass I had enough (barely) to feed the four of us and forego the peanut butter pasta. I then and there decided to learn more about what was in the lakes of the Boundary Waters and that was the beginning of this book.

With all the lakes in this wonderful area, even if you have fished it for years, there is no way one could know them all. Nights spent pouring over maps only serve to set the fishing juices flowing. It is a marvelous thing to have a vivid imagination but does little to improve your fishing.

Because there are so many lakes in the Canoe Country and because much of the time we are only on a particular lake for a short time, many do not do the research necessary to find out just what is in the lake or what it is like.

Any of us who frequent the area probably have a favorite lake or two. Not because these lakes are exceptional fishing lakes. Many times it is just because we are familiar and comfortable with the lake. Our trips are valuable to us and we don't want to waste time in an area that may not be up to par. Finding out about other lakes is not always easy. Even the best of friends will lie straight faced about a good lake that you have asked about. For those who do not live in the immediate area surrounding the BWCAW, there are no friendly bait shops to give hints and the nearest Fisheries Office of the DNR may not be known to them.

These then are the reasons for this book. Too much of modern fishing literature is centered on hi-tech fishing techniques. This guide will tell you the basics about both the lakes you will encounter and the habits of the fish. It hopes to inform the reader about the tackle requirements for the changing lakes and species you will fish for as you paddle through and how to put the kit together so that it is still portable.

It won't make you a fishing expert. The range and depth of such a book, if possible at all, would be enormous. Nor do you need to be an expert to catch fish in the Canoe Country. You don't need a degree in limnology or have to own all the latest in electronic fishing paraphernalia to catch fish. This approach to fishing is too "hawg fish" oriented, especially for the Canoe Country.

Knowing how to read a lake, where to look for fish, what their habits are and how to present the lure are far more important than all the edges modern equipment and do-dads may profess to give. Hopefully this guide book will verse you upon these basics, teach you a little something about the lakes and their fish.

When I first fished the Canoe Country with my father many years ago our success was sometimes fantastic. It still can be. It is one of the major reasons I return there as often as I do. The pristine lakes and bountiful fish are relatively unchanged and the country offers greater rewards than numbers of dead fish. Maybe, armed with the basic tackle and knowledge we need we can all take a fishing trip back into what still is the "good old days." I hope you find this book a valuable aid in catching a fine mess of fish.

Chapter Two

What to Take With You and Why

GOING INTO THE CANOE COUNTRY without a fishing rod would be like going on your honeymoon without your new spouse. It might still be enjoyable, but not nearly so. Yet every year I see people on the portages, tramping by under their bug nets, with no rod in sight. Some may choose to forgo fishing because of a sincere lack of interest. Therapy can help these sad folks. Others may not know what to bring or be unsure of how, when or where to fish the wilderness. They should buy this book.

Fishing these beautiful northwoods lakes does not require a large investment in equipment. If you fish for the same or similar fish at home, chances are you already have most of the stuff you'll need. The trick is in knowing what to haul along, what you must have, especially if you are unfamiliar with this area. There are no bait shops in the interior. What is in your pack when you enter will have to serve throughout the trip.

It pays then, to give your tackle needs some serious consideration before you leave home. A little homework can save you consternation in the field. Invariably you will find that you could have used a few more of this and a lot less of that. Remember, you are not fishing from a bass boat with three tackle boxes at your feet. You must select carefully your tackle requirements. In the Canoe Country lugging all the unnecessary items along can be a very real pain in the back. Your equipment should be easily packed and relatively light in weight. It has been said that if your tackle box has handles, or more than one tray, you have too much stuff. Ideally your equipment, except for your rod, should fit in your pack. This leaves your hands free on the portages for swatting mosquitoes. Weight and space are never more important as when you are on a canoe trip or backpacking.

The first item to consider is your rod. Just about any style will do. If you prefer a casting rod to spinning, that's fine. Just make sure you are familiar and comfortable with it. I have found from experience and by interviewing others that the most popular rod for this wilderness is a 6½ to 7 foot, medium action spinning rod. With it, of course, would go a light to medium action spinning reel.

Your rod can be carried in a rod case or exposed. There are advantages to both and each traveler must decide which way he prefers.

A rod case will protect the rod from damage both in the canoe and on portages. This can be important because a broken fishing rod in the middle of your trip can make any further fishing difficult if not impossible. The single disadvantage is that, given human nature, one is less likely to keep the rod ready to fish as you pass through lakes from one portage to the next. Many fish have been caught by trolling a lure behind the canoe as you travel. And although this is an unscientific approach, remember that you can't catch fish unless your lure is in the water.

Everything you need for all your Canoe Country fishing should fit in a small tackle box.

Some who like to keep their rod out of a case prefer a slightly shorter rod, say about 5¹/2 to 6 feet, but still of a medium action. They feel the shorter rod is easier to handle on portages and takes less room in the canoe while still being strung, baited and ready for action. Longer rods can be broken down into two pieces while still strung, being careful not to tangle or nick the line, and the two halves bound together with a rubber band or two.

In either case the rod is simply carried, ready to fish, across the portage or is stuck up in the bow of the canoe. The same can be done to rods in cases or either can be taped to the thwarts. Remember to keep the weight of anything attached to the canoe in equal balance side to side and front to back. This will make the canoe much easier to portage. The advantage of not using a case for your rod is that it is more likely you will have it out and ready to fish when you need it.

Although some folks like the four and five piece pack rods, I would stay with a set up as described for the same reason as keeping your rod out of a case. The little pack rods are very nice as far as space saving goes but require even more time to put together and take apart. Being a basically lazy person I have found that pack rods greatly inhibit the prospects of my taking a cast or two into fishy looking cover as we travel through. When it is windy or the bugs are really bad the last thing you want to be doing is fiddling around trying to assemble such a rod.

Your choice in rod material can be of either of the standards, those being fiberglass or graphite. The latter tend to be more expensive and you may want to think twice about carrying them across this rugged country. While I have never broken a rod while in the Boundary Waters, I have flattened a few guides and put some nice nicks in the rod itself. Not that I recommend using a cheap rod. These seldom hold up under the best of conditions let alone a trip into a wilderness area. Just make sure you take a sturdy rod in sound shape. If you feel uncomfortable using your expensive new graphite rod, take along your older but still in good shape back-up rod.

The reel should likewise be functional and should be matched to the rod. By this I mean a spinning reel on a spinning rod and a medium duty reel for a medium duty rod. Make sure the reel is working properly. Go over it, tightening the screws and giving it a few drops of oil, if needed. Now is the time to find any problems and take care of them. A loose bail spring that just sunk out of sight in Little Saganaga Lake can cause a similar reaction in your chest.

The reel should be spooled with six to ten pound line. Your experience as a fisherman will determine how light a line you should use. The lighter the line the easier it will cast and with greater distance. It will also be less visible to the fish. There are very few fish that can't be landed on six pound line. If you have little fishing experience, go with eight or ten pound line. You will have more confidence while fighting fish and will lose fewer lures to snags. Your line should be new and of a premium brand. If you use a spinning reel you can take along a spare spool already wound with line. If you like, take along a refill spool of line as it comes packaged from the store. This will allow you to wind it on your reel or anyone else's should the need arise. A one hundred to two hundred yard spool should be more than enough. You might want to include a small leader spool for making bait rigs or you can use the line from your reel. The best bet is to make these up at home and have them ready to go. In any case the line for these rigs need not be any heavier than what is on your reel, though you may want it lighter should the water be clear and the fish finicky.

To the great delight of fishing equipment manufacturers, fishermen love all kinds of gadgets designed for their sport. Most of these toys are unnecessary and should be left at home. You can forget about all your sophisticated electronic paraphernalia. It is impractical to drag this stuff all over the Canoe Country and for the most part, not needed. You don't really want to know the water's pH factor or dissolved oxygen content anyway, do you? One of the small, basic depth finders might be taken with you if you feel it necessary but a topographic map of the lake will probably serve you as well and fit in your shirt pocket. Some of the commercial BWCAW maps have depth soundings of the lakes that have been sounded and the same is true of the U.S. Geological Survey maps. Not all of the lakes have been sounded but these are, for the most part, small lakes and should be easily scouted out by yourself.

For those venturing into the Quetico, you'll find your options limited. Few Quetico lakes have been surveyed and so you'll find little contour information on maps. You are on your own when exploring these remote jewels. If your canoe trip revolves solely around fishing, the addition of a portable fish locator may be worth your effort.

There are, however, some things that could be considered a must for your trip. One should always have a good knife handy while fishing. Both a fillet knife and a pocket knife should be on hand. The fillet knife, of course, is for cleaning and filleting your fish. It should have a flexible blade of six inches or more in length. Since fillet knives need to be razor sharp to do a proper job, and since they do dull easily, some means of sharpening the knife should be included in your kit. A small steel, mini-crock sticks or a small whetstone will do. The whetstone will also allow you to keep your hooks sharp. A fillet knife should be sharpened about every other fish, any longer between sharpenings will leave you with a blunted edge that will make sharpening very difficult.

A good pocket knife can also be considered a necessity. Besides the uses you will find for it around camp it is handy while fishing to trim the ends from knots or cutting out snarls. While you could use your fillet knife for this, it dulls it needlessly and the long blade can be unwieldy for smaller tasks. Make sure both knives are as sharp as possible before leaving home; it will keep your sharpening time to a minimum in the field.

A few other tools should be taken along as well. A needle nose pliers is a must for removing hooks from toothy mouths. They will save you countless cuts to your fingers and more importantly, allow you to quickly release uninjured and unwanted fish to the water. A lot of people don't bother to take along a landing net, myself included. They have a nasty habit of getting caught in everything on portages and since you will be releasing many of your fish (you can only eat so many and there is no way to keep them for days) it is a simple matter to grasp the hook with the pliers and twist it free, all while the water supports the fish.

Smallmouth bass can be lifted into the canoe by firmly grasping their lower jaws between thumb and forefinger. Their teeth are small and pose no problem. This grasp paralyzes them for a time until you can remove the hooks. If the fish is to be released, do it quickly and while the fish is still partially in the water. All other fish can be handled by sliding your hand back to their midsection, again while they are still in the lake, and lifting slightly. At this point you can remove the hook or stick it on the stringer. Don't grab a fish by the eye sockets or gills if it is to be released or even if you want to keep it alive on the stringer as this will surely kill or blind the fish.

For those fish you wish to keep, a stringer of some type will be needed. The long cord type stringers are the easiest and most foolproof of all. Simple to use, they seldom break and often find themselves doing double duty as a handy hunk of rope. The long ones, six feet or more, allow the fish to stay in deeper, cooler water. This is helpful in keeping them from going belly up on hot days. They are also nice for tying to a bush or tree on shore and still making it possible for the fish to get into deeper water. This is important if you plan on trying to keep a few fish alive for tomorrow's breakfast.

Never cram a lot of fish on one stringer if you plan on keeping them alive for any amount of time. If you do try to keep them overnight, I have found that two or three fish are about the maximum on one stringer. Cord stringers are light, cheap and last indefinitely so you might want to consider throwing a couple in the pack. It is nice to have one at each end of the canoe so you don't have to toss fish from one end to the other.

Other possible niceties would include a hook hone, a de-liar scale for the curious or honest, a portage anchor and attendant rope and a burlap sack.

Portage anchors are a simple nylon mesh bag with a drawstring top and a brass ring to tie to. They resemble a heavy duty hair net and can be purchased or easily made. These handy anchors weigh almost nothing until filled with rocks and roll up to be quite small. It makes the task of locating an anchor a simple one because if there is one thing the Canoe Country has plenty of, it is rocks. You should not under estimate the importance of an anchor for fishing. Add some parachute cord and you have a nice, light anchor line.

The burlap sack is for keeping fish fresh and cool. Placing fish in a thoroughly soaked bag will maintain a steady temperature, cool enough to keep them fresh for a day or more. This should be enough time to get them to the next camp or back to the car. Nothing more than a variation of the old desert water bag trick, just make sure you hang the sack up in the shade.

Your tackle needs will be based on what species of fish you are after and to a certain extent, how serious you are. Some individuals will be willing to carry a bit more than others. But keep in mind that this is one case where more is not always better. A lot of tackle is interchangeable from one species to the next. A smaller portion is more specific in nature. Of course, if your trip is centered on just one species, your tackle can be tailored for it.

We will get into specific needs in the chapters on each fish. The following list of tackle is a suggestion based upon the premise that you want to try for all of major Canoe Country species. All of the tackle listed are tried and true favorites of the area and while you may not see some of your favorites on the list, a tackle box filled with these or similar ingredients will see you through very nicely.

- hooks, bait type with short shank in sizes six to four. Bring plenty, minimum of twenty-five.
- sinkers, split shot, slip sinkers and a few bead chain keel sinkers for trolling. Bring a range of split shot, $^1/8$ to $^1/2$ ounce in the slip and keel sinkers. For deep water trolling during midsummer you'll want some 1 to 3 ounce weights.
- swivels, snap type, two and three way types.
- floating jig heads and corkies in orange, chartreuse and red.
- jigs, hair and feather types. $^1/8$ to $^1/4$ ounce size in yellow, orange, chartreuse, red and white. For lake trout throw in a few $^1/2$ to 1 ounce jigs in yellow, white, black, red/white and black/white.
- rubber bodied jigs, with and without spinner blades such as Ugly Bugs, Mr. Twisters and Fuzzee Grubs. Best colors seem to be chartreuse, yellow, black, brown and purple. $^1/8$ to $^3/8$ ounce. Take along extra bodies.
- plugs, both surface and diving. Diving plugs such as the Rapalas and Lazy Ikes and surface plugs like the Rapalas, Heddon Torpedo and the Jitterbug. Trolling plugs can be two to five inches in length, surface plugs for smallmouth should be no longer than 1 $^1/2$ to 2 inches. Smallmouth will want small plugs. Colors best in silver, gold, blue, orange and perch.
- spinners, such as the Mepps and Vibrax in sizes 1 and 2. Silver or gold blades and with or without squirrel tails.
- spoons, both heavy for casting and light for trolling ("flutter spoons"). $^1/2$ to $^7/8$ ounce in silver, gold, hammered brass, gold/orange and red/white. For deep water vertical jigging for lake

25

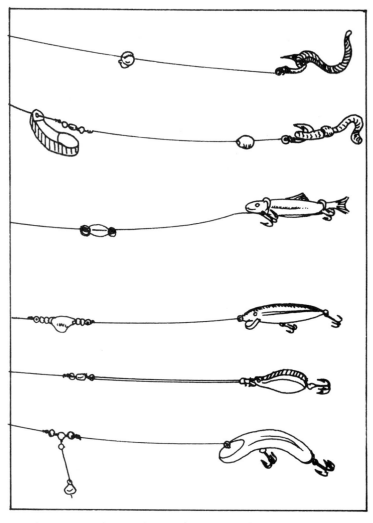

Popular and simple bait and lure rigs for all around fishing are, top to bottom:
- *Short shank hook and splitshot for leeches or worms*
- *A slip sinker, swivel and corkie for floating bait off bottom*
- *minnow harness and sinker for bottom still fishing*
- *keel sinker with built-in swivel for keeping line twist to a minimum while trolling with plugs or spoons*
- *steel leader and spoon for northern pike fishing*
- *three-way swivel with dropper (1-3 feet) and heavy sinker for deep water trolling*

trout, some ½ and 1 ounce Heddon Sonars.
- a couple of bobbers, slip type preferably.
- poppers, both hair and cork, for the flyfisherman. Best sizes for smallmouth are 8, 6, and 4. Some eelworm and muddler streamers and a few dry ties.

At first glance this may sound like a lot of tackle but once assembled you should find that it will pack quite small and portageable. When concentrating on one type of fishing on a trip you can beef up that area, eliminate others. You should also find that the bulk of your equipment will be made up of the smaller lures and things rather than large plugs and the like.

All of your tackle except the pliers, rolled up stringer and the fillet knife should fit into one small box. Some anglers, myself included, may prefer those flat tackle boxes that are about the size of a cigar box. In fact an old cigar box can work well. If you have need of more space than this you probably have too much stuff.

A box like this will sit nicely under the top flap of a Duluth pack, no matter how stuffed it already is. You want to keep the tackle, as well as the rod, accessible so that you won't hesitate to take a few casts as you paddle along.

What about live bait? Well, it is a fact that live bait can improve your fishing success. At times, when the fish are finicky, live bait may be the only thing that will work. That doesn't mean you must have it. If all you have are artificial lures and you know how to use them, you'll catch fish. But bait will give you an advantage.

Live bait does not always travel well and it is always an added nuisance. Only you can decide if it is worth your time and effort. However, there are baits that travel better than others and there are also frozen, salted and freeze dried baits. The preserved baits can take the place of live baits when they are used for bottom fishing or tipping an artificial lure.

The two live baits that get the nod for ease in transporting and care are leeches and worms. These are primarily bass and walleye baits. Both are easy to carry, even in large numbers, and are simple to care for. They are also pretty much interchangeable although fish can show a preference toward one on certain days or seasons. Generally, fish will take leeches better during the spring than they will worms.

The major enemy of both baits is heat. If you can keep them cool, and change the leech's water frequently, you'll be able to keep them squirming throughout your trip. A small styrofoam cooler, six pack size, is perfect for this. Put the leeches into a sturdy plastic bag before putting them in the cooler and seal with a twist-tie or rubber band. This will allow you to set the cooler in the pack without leaking on the macaroni and cheese. If you have it available, throw in a little ice at the beginning of the trip. Any amount of cooling you can do to the leeches or worms at the start will just extend their life that much further into the trip. Whether in camp or canoe, keep the bait in the shade as nothing will cook them faster than the sun.

I've found that a wide-mouth, plastic water bottle is a handy container for transporting leeches. They are tough and leakproof. Once used for this purpose, though, you had better label it so you can tell it apart from your other bottles. Lemonade mixed in one of these bottles has a very distinctive flavor.

Minnows are another matter entirely. They require frequent changes of water and also must be kept cool. Minnow buckets are large and cumbersome, have a tendency to spill and splash as well as being a general nuisance on portages. Those of you planning on covering a lot of territory may decide that minnows are not worth the effort.

If you are going to be setting up a base camp and traveling from there taking along minnows may be less of a prob-

Oxygen packs will help make transporting minnows easier and keep them alive longer.

lem. Have your bait dealer put your minnows in an oxygen pack. An oxygen pack is nothing more than a very heavy plastic bag into which the minnows and a small amount of water are placed. It is then pumped full of pure oxygen and sealed with a rubber band. Packed like this, and kept cool and unopened, the minnows will keep for up to three or four days. This gives you enough time to reach a base camp after which the minnows can be put into a minnow bucket and submerged in the lake. Another twist is to have the oxygen packs filled with a day or two's worth of minnows, only opening the packs, one at a time, as you need them. Minnows cannot be taken into the Quetico.

If live minnows are not a necessity or you are entering the Quetico, an alternative would be to take freeze-dried or salted minnows. These keep indefinitely and are more than adequate for bottom fishing for lake trout and northern. They also work well for trolling or for tipping a spoon or jig since this normally requires hooking a minnow through the head, a process that kills the bait anyway.

The best all around live minnow to take is the fathead chub. They are hardy and available in a range of sizes. Chubs work well on just about any species of fish that you may be after. Sucker minnows are also a good bet and the large sizes are the preferred bait for big northerns and lake trout. When using preserved bait try shiner minnows or smelt. Shiners are just about impossible to keep alive anyway but are very effective bait. Smelt are generally not available in any other form. Both are deadly on lake trout and northerns.

Why bother with minnows at all? Early and late in the season the predator fish feed heavily on minnows and minnows at this time of year are bound to work for you. It is generally cooler then as well, making caring for the minnows an easier task. If your trip will be in the heat of the summer you can probably leave the minnows behind but a trip in the spring or fall might just prove that they are worth the effort.

Whatever bait you choose to use remember these points. Live or preserved bait can increase your fishing success. All live bait must be kept cool and some require frequent changes in water. Try to put them in sturdy containers and if possible, try to fit them in your pack in order to keep hassles along the portages to a minimum.

Should you decide to take no live bait along, do not despair. With the selection of lures discussed and the knowledge to use them, you should find that consistent catches of fish are not too difficult. Regardless of what types of baits and lures you take remember to give it a little thought and consideration. Check that rod and reel over and then get ready. You're about to head into some of the finest fishing country God ever laid his hand to.

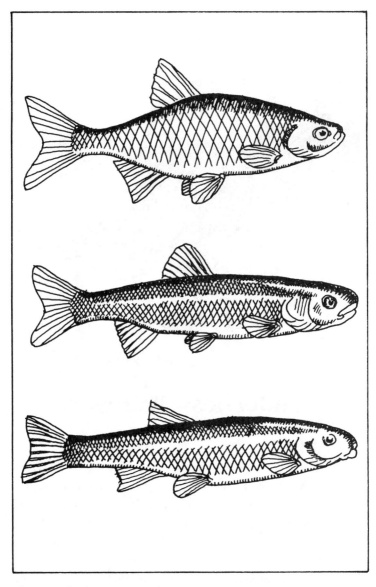

Three popular bait minnows, top to bottom: Shiner, Fathead chub and Sucker. All are effective but shiners can be hard to keep alive.

Chapter 3

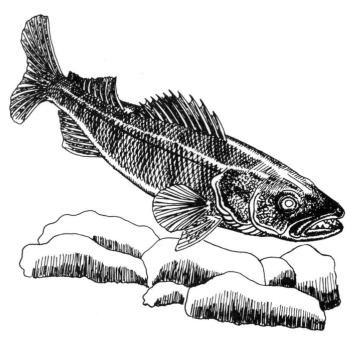

Wilderness Walleyes

THE MOST SOUGHT AFTER FISH in Minnesota, the walleye is equally popular within the Boundary Waters. The largest member of the perch family, it is not pursued because of any legendary fighting prowess. The most fighting involved with walleyes is who is going to get the last fillet from the frying pan. For this is the real basis of the walleye's popularity, it is delectable dinner fare.

Not that some aren't respectable on the end of a rod. It's just that they aren't very memorable either. Many a big walleye has been mistaken for a snag being retrieved from the bottom, much to the surprise of the fisherman when he sees those big, luminous eyes coming up toward him.

I suspect that the rest of their popularity comes from the fact that the average walleye, around a couple of pounds, is fairly easy to catch. True, there are times during the year when catching walleyes can be a downright mystery, but for the most part they are fairly predictable. Consistently catching above average size walleyes is another matter entirely.

This receives a lot of attention by those "pro" fishermen and they often raise a lot of hullabaloo while trying to make a science of walleye fishing. You have your backtrolling, oxygen meters, temperature gauges and video sonar. You have your "haws" walleyes, structure, weedlines and the rest of the terminology. And you get your fill of mesotrophic, eutrophic and myopic lake types. Of course, you have a bass boat with two outboard motors and an electric trolling motor, all of this to catch a meal of walleyes and most of which means diddly-squat for the wilderness canoeing fisherman.

The truth of the matter is that with a little common sense, the ability to read water, maybe a topographic map of the lake and some basic background on the likes, dislikes and habits of walleyes you can do a respectable job of catching your dinner. The other half is that even if you wanted to you would not be able to take most of the aforementioned gear along anyway, either by law (no motors) or the fact that it is just too much to lug around on your back.

Many of the lakes in the BWCAW and Quetico are crawling with walleyes. There are lots of large walleyes up there and the Minnesota state record fish came from Saganaga Lake. This monster weighed in at 17 pounds, 8 ounces. Each year many fish are taken in the ten pound range. Any walleye over six pounds is a big fish and the "keeper" fish start at about a pound and a half.

Big walleyes can be taken in this area, even if you don't know what you are doing! I'm proof of that. My father hauled me into the outback one June for a little walleye fishing. We were joined by my brother Butch, who was a popular fishing guide in the area at that time and a buddy of his who was also taking money for fishing under the poor pretense of doing it for a living.

We were on one of those large border lakes, Butch selecting the lake because of its reputation for nice fish, and we had lashed the two canoes together with popple poles making a veritable catamaran. They told me that this was for greater stability on the large water but I now suspect it may have been because, at eight years old, I was not much help in handling a canoe. Butch and I were in the one canoe, my dad and the other guide in the second.

Two things stand out in my mind about that day. One was the fact that the mosquitoes were large and plentiful. "So big," my father said, "that they had woodticks on them." The other memory centered around my brand new fishing rod that my father proudly produced after work the night before we left. It was one of those new fangled fiberglass jobs with a push button spincasting reel. My previous rod had been made of steel. The reel came all loaded with monofilament line that must have been about one hundred pound test. With the solid glass rod and the heavy line I could cast about thirty feet. There was no way I could hang a lure in the trees along shore with that rig, a thought that may have crossed my father's mind when he selected it. In any case, I thought it was beautiful.

We were trolling along with a new secret bait Butch had discovered. It was a balsa wood minnow, silver in color and about four inches long, straight from Finland. Later, someone was to make a couple of zillion dollars marketing these things under the name of Rapala. True to the form of serious

34

fishermen (or dense) we were not concerned with how much money the lure might make for someone, we just knew they caught fish. The lure was called a Talus.

As the innumerable spruce trees slid past the slow moving canoes, each one harboring equally uncountable mosquitoes, my rod doubled over. I yanked on that thing as hard as I could, only to feel it stop dead. "Fish?" asked Butch. "Naw, only a snag," I returned. To my chagrin the line started to cut through the water away from the canoe. It was, indeed, a fish. The battle on, it soon became obvious that this was not just a fish, but a large one. After a couple of minutes of my reeling against the drag, the rod tip under the canoe and my relentless pumping of the rod, my father, in the next canoe if you remember, told my brother to take the rod away from me. The fish was too big for me to handle. I didn't know any swear words at that age, but if I had, I'm sure I would have used a few choice ones at that point, father or no father.

To my undying gratitude Butch said, "No, let him handle it, he's got to learn to fight his own big fish."

With the hundred pound line, the stiff glass rod, and two sets of treble hooks, my father needn't have worried. I think I cranked that walleye right up to the top guide of the doubled over rod. Butch told me to work it back toward him and with his help, like a derrick, I swung that fish through the air into the canoe. This fish just was destined to be mine.

Flopping around in the bottom of the canoe, the fish was only surpassed in size by the roundness of my eyes. On the stringer finally, Butch passed it up to me to inspect. I tied that stringer to the canoe seat with about twelve knots, and lowered him over the side. I really don't remember much about what the rest of the party was doing at that point or for the rest of the day. I spent the next five hours or so bent over the canoe, watching my fish, making sure it didn't get away. When we weighed it later that day it neared nine pounds. Despite all the things that could have gone wrong, this old moss backed, marble eyed monster was mine. And if an eight year old can do it, so can you. Walleyes, also known as *Stizostedian vilreum vitreum*, prefer larger bodies of water. They are identified by their light colored belly, olive green or brassy sides, six or seven dark bands crossing their back and a milk white tip to the bottom of their tail. However, some Canoe Country lakes contain walleyes that are almost black on the sides, possibly the result of isolated genetics, living in deep, dark water or the combination of both. Mary Jo and I have found a few places in the Quetico where the walleyes have a very distinctive blue coloration. In any case, you can't miss those marble sized, pale glowing eyes for which the fish are named.

These big eyes can tell us something important. Walleyes are very light sensitive. They feed primarily at dawn and dusk and bright, calm days are usually poor for fishing. Overcast days with a slight chop on the water to cut down the light penetration will invariably help your walleye fishing. It even goes to the extreme that walleyes will be found on the shady side of reefs and can go up or down the reef with the angle and penetration of the sun.

Walleyes are even night spawners. They spawn in the spring, just after ice-out, and the dates for this event fluctuate with the weather of that particular year. In the BWCAW spawning occurs near the Minnesota general fishing opener.

Walleyes spawn in rivers or on lake shoals where there is wind and wave action. When they spawn they will be highly concentrated. They are also very susceptible to a lure at this time and the combination of both sometimes forces the DNR to close areas to fishing in order to allow the fish to spawn unmolested. Most of the spawning will occur when the water temperature reaches 45 to 50 degrees. At this time of year many big fish are landed and these are almost always females, the males being much smaller.

It often happens that the walleye spawning has just ended when the fishing season opens. The opener is the first trip of the year for many wanderers in the Boundary Waters. This can be a very fruitless experience because the fishing for walleyes after they have spawned is almost the worst of the year. It seems that they feed very little during this time and are also quite scattered as they move back to their traditional summer haunts. When this occurs I recommend that you go lake trout fishing. It is at its best at this time.

Now the "pros" term this the "post-spawn period" and have tried to figure out all kinds of things you can do in order to catch walleyes at this time. I still recommend that you go lake trout fishing. But if you insist on fishing for walleyes when they aren't feeding, you can try a couple of things.

Walleyes like warm water and chances are you will have your best luck by looking for them in parts of the lake that warm up more quickly than the rest, i.e., shallow bays and shores. Even this warmer water is likely to be below their preferred temperature, so fish slowly. Walleyes are methodical, deliberate feeders and when the water is cold they will be even slower. These shallow bays are sometimes very muddy bottomed, generally a no-no in walleye fishing since they like hard bottoms. There may well be, however, some gravel or a rock pile amidst that warm muddy bay. That is where the walleyes would be. They also like to feed on insect larvae during the early part of the season and these are hatched in areas like this. With a rock pile near by to home in on, they can make feeding forays into the insect laden areas.

Walleye fishing is at its best when this slow period ends and they have again set up shop for the summer on their favorite reef or shoal. These prime locations are characteristic in nature. They generally have abrupt changes in their topography, are near deep water and are rocky. Stay away from mucky bottoms; walleyes like hard bottoms, be they sand, gravel or rubble.

During the first month in which the walleyes have returned to their summer haunts, the fish will be in fairly shallow water. By shallow I mean in the range of five to fifteen feet. The factors that will influence at exactly what depth the fish will be found should be carefully examined when you begin fishing. These factors include water clarity, temperature, amount of sunlight and direction and strength of the wind. The time of day can also affect the fish's behavior.

Remember walleyes are very light conscious. A bright day on a very clear lake will likely mean fairly deep fish, even early in the season. The same day and lake, with a slight chop to the water will probably bring the fish up. During the same bright day, with or without a wind, the morning and evening are bound to be better times to be fishing. Unless you're a real diehard you might as well put up the hammock and read a book during the middle of bright, calm days.

To be on the safe side during your early summer, late spring fishing trips, start looking for walleyes in about five feet of water. Unless the day is extremely dark, the water exceptionally murky or its temperature very cold, the fish are not likely to be shallower than that. However, their habits are not always predictable and there are times when they could be right up next to shore, so be flexible.

At any time of year you will want to look for walleyes over rocky reefs, shoals and points. These types of structures are pretty easy to spot just by examining the lake's shoreline. Watch for rubbly beaches and points and then examine the water off these. You want to determine if this same type of rocky nature is carried out into the lake. If there is a topographic

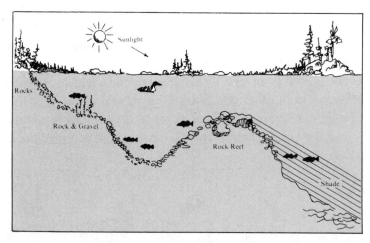

Walleyes will use different structures and locations depending on the weather, time of day or season. Early season or summer mornings and evenings may find them shallow over weeds and hard bottoms; overcast days with a chop on the water in summer may find them at a moderate depth near rocky drop-offs; bright, calm days often move them to the shady side of reefs or points.

map of your lake available it can save you some time by directing you to likely looking areas.

There are a lot of Boundary Water and Quetico lakes that have never been sounded, however. In that case the information listed in this book can be of some help. By comparing the maximum depth with the littoral percentage (the percent of the lake's area less than fifteen feet in depth) you can formulate a rude mental picture of the lake. For example, if the lake has a maximum depth of thirty-five feet and eighty percent of it is less than fifteen feet deep you can probably infer that most of the deep water is located in one, possibly two, small holes. This lake is not a likely candidate for having myriads of reefs and sunken islands. Most of the structure is probably near the deep hole with the remainder being on shorelines with the proper bottom. After visually examining the lake and with this background information, you can begin to make some informed choices as to where to start fishing.

It is helpful at times to make your own soundings. This can be simply done by bouncing a heavy jig along the bottom as you crisscross an area. By keeping your line tight and paying attention to the feel you can get an accurate picture of the bottom contours and what it is made up of. Paddle slowly or use the wind. There is also the chance that you may hook a fish.

The lack of a fish locator doesn't mean you can't find hidden structure. By padding or drifting with the wind and bouncing a heavy jig along the bottom you can find deeper reefs, whether looking for walleyes or lake trout, while at the same time perhaps hooking a fish.

Walleyes feed on the bottom and are schooling fish, two points that are in the fisherman's favor. Except at certain odd times of the year when walleyes will suspend far off the bottom in order to find the right combination of water temperature and oxygen, they will be right down amidst the rocks. Once you find one down there, chances are you'll find more.

The most popular method for locating fish is by trolling. In the Canoe Country this means a lot of paddling. By trolling you can cover a lot of water in a relatively short amount of time. If you do locate fish, that is you catch one, mark the spot immediately. This can be done with a small buoy or by making visual triangulations with landmarks on shore. You could also ease out the anchor. It is important to quickly mark the spot because of the walleye's schooling habit. Too many fishermen consider the happy chance of catching a fish just that, a chance, and then continue blissfully on their way. Mark that spot!

When trolling, the best lures are minnow imitating plugs like the Rapala or Lazy Ike. These plugs should be about three to six inches in length and the best colors are silver, gold or perch-like finishes. I've found that floating plugs have better action than the sinking models and would advise using a floater with a sinker, if necessary, over the sinking models. A small bead chain swivel sinker three feet or so from the lure works best and helps to keep line twist to a minimum. In a pinch, split shot can be used.

A slow trolling speed for walleyes is important. Most fishermen troll too quickly and this results in many fewer strikes. On a day with little or no wind, one person paddling slowly is about the right speed. If wind makes it necessary for both to paddle, keep it as slow as you can and still be able to maintain control of the canoe. If it is windy enough, and the wind is blowing in the right direction, try using the wind as your trolling motor. This can be very effective.

Try to troll parallel to reefs and points. One pass is not always enough if the cover looks good. You may have to experiment a little with the depth and speed which may seem time consuming. In the long run, though, enticing fish near you to strike is a lot quicker than chasing greener pastures, especially when you have to paddle to get to them. If the structure is right, there should be fish on it somewhere and patience will win out.

Because paddling for endless hours can be wearing, take the opportunity to use the wind if it presents itself. Let it drift

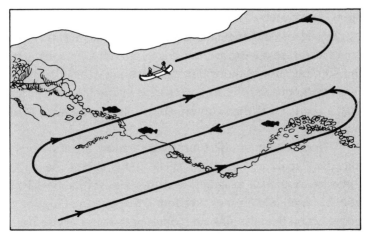

Troll slowly parallel to reefs and points. Several passes may be needed to determine proper depth.

you over likely looking areas and bounce a jig along, or if going very slowly, cast with a countdown type plug. By bouncing a jig along you kill two birds with one stone. As mentioned before, you are sounding out the bottom, the tick-tick-tick of the jig on the bottom can give you an idea of what the bottom looks like and how hard it is. At the same time you stand a good chance of catching a walleye. It is best to plan your drift to run parallel to the structure, or quartering it, rather than quickly up one side and down the other.

There may be times when you wish to both travel quickly and troll. For years it bothered me that we were passing over what was obviously prime fishing waters but unable to spend any time fishing them. Sure, you could troll, but the fact is most fishing lures do not run well at the faster speeds one might reach when really cruising along. In the last few years, however, I've found a type of plug that will allow you to both travel and troll quickly.

These plugs are known as "no-bill" crankbaits. Some popular brands are the Cotton Cordell Rattlin' Spot, Bill Lewis Rat-L-Trap and the Rapala's Rattlin' Rap. The half ounce size seems to be the best all around and I've had my best luck on perch-like colors and the basic black/silver combination. These tear-drop shaped plugs are very thin and will not twist or spin when pulled at high speeds. They are a sinking lure so that little weight needs to be added if you are fishing in five feet of water or less. A keel sinker four feet up the line will allow you to fish deeper waters, up to about fifteen feet, depending upon the weight of the sinker you've attached.

By removing the front set of treble hooks (which I do to all my plugs, not just these) you will reduce the number of snags. These plugs, and most others, run with the nose down. Since the rear hook is riding high and behind the lure, and the front treble has been removed, a plug can bounce bottom very frequently without hanging up. I've not noticed any missed strikes by removing these hooks since a fish hitting a trolled lure really hits hard, usually causing a near certain hook-up. I have noticed, though, fewer hooks in fingers and pant legs. Fish are almost always hooked by the rear gang of trebles anyway, leaving the front ones to flop ominously about. You'll also find releasing fish easier if these excess hooks are missing. Don't worry, removing the hooks doesn't seem to impede the lure's action.

The rare snag occurs when the lure swims into a rock pile and becomes wedged. These can usually be removed by reversing your direction. This bottom bouncing technique is critical for walleye success and is also effective on northern pike and smallmouth bass. The same lure and high speed trolling technique is also effective on spring lake trout when they are cruising over shallow reefs.

This technique is probably no one's first choice in fishing methods but, when done on those days when you'll spend most of your time traveling, will provide many bonus fish and supply some dinners. It is helpful to modify your route, if convenient, to pass near points of land, near islands or along shore to put you in likely fish habitat. You'll also need to prop your rod within reaching distance and in a manner that does not allow it to be pulled backward or overboard. These "no-bill" crankbaits put a pretty fair bend in your rod when you reach top speed and you'll also need to be prepared for the eventual strike or snag.

Don't panic if your lure bounces bottom and the rod tip swings back. Leave your drag set lightly in the event you truly hang up. Most of the time you'll find that the lure has only briefly touched bottom but not gotten snagged. Believe me, I've worn the front end clean off of many plugs without losing them to the lake bottom. By keeping the lure in close proximity of the bottom, you'll greatly increase the number of strikes you'll receive.

Hopefully after drift fishing or trolling for a while you will have tied into a fish or two and marked the spot. Because walleyes are such slow feeders it is nearly always preferable to fish from a stationary craft. You can better control the depth of your bait, get a superior feel of the bottom and allow the fish the time to play with the bait, if using live bait.

It is hard at times to beat live bait for walleye fishing because of their slow pick up. Live bait will allow them the luxury of toying with it for a minute or two, a practice that generally will result in more hooked fish. You may not wish to haul live bait along however. In that case you can still do well with artificials.

Probably the best artificials for still fishing for walleyes are jigs. Feather, hair or rubber bodied jigs work very well and each type has their devotees. I've not found a tremendous difference in the success of each type over all, but on some days there can be a dramatic preference for one type. To be safe, carry some of each. The best colors are red, yellow, white, chartreuse and orange in about a ¹/4 ounce size. Some jigs come with a spinner blade above the body. These also work very well and the blade sometimes helps to attract reluctant fish.

Rubber bodied jigs often come with, or have available for them, replacement bodies. These are a handy item to take along and cost little in space or weight. They allow you to replace a torn body or to change colors without having to retie the entire rig, just by threading a new body on the hook.

If you do have live bait available it is often helpful to tip the jig with a minnow, leech or piece of worm. Sometimes this combination works when neither alternative will. Since leeches and worms travel easier than do live minnows they often get the nod as the canoeist's bait. Leeches catch walleyes from opening day of the fishing season on, with the worms catching up in the summer. Minnows inflows are at their best in the spring and fall. Look in Chapter Two for information on types of minnows and how to care for and transport all types of live and preserved bait.

Live bait rigs for walleyes are very simple. The best type are the "Lindy" rigs which can be purchased or made by yourself. The hook size should be small and short shanked. A bait hook in a size six should suffice for any bait except large minnows or for bottom fishing with big, dead minnows. For this a minnow harness should be used.

When using a small bait hook, the sinker should be placed about a foot and a half to three feet above. This can be a medium split shot or a slip sinker. Slip sinkers allow the fish to pick up the bait and run a distance with it, a favorite trick of walleyes, before stopping to swallow it. Because the line slips through the sinker the fish feels no resistance. In order to keep the sinker the proper distance from the hook a tiny swivel is tied in to act as a stopper. A quicker method is

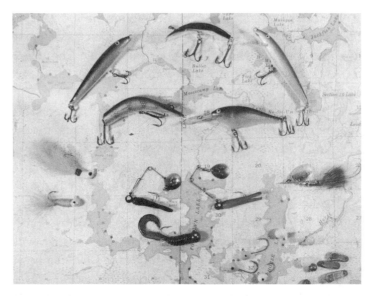

Tried and true walleye lures: plugs, two floating Rapalas, two Lazy Ikes and a diving Rapala; jigs, both rubber bodied and hair or feather; Mepps spinner and corkies, floating jig heads, hooks and sinkers for live bait.

to use one of those teeny little split shot on the line to stop the slip sinker. Slip sinkers for walleyes should be about $1/4$ to $1/8$ ounce.

Other handy items for live bait fishing are floating jig heads and corkies. Floating jig heads look like jigs but keep your bait off the bottom with their cork or foam head. Corkies do the same but are small balls that slide down to your hook, allowing you to use the same bait rig. Many live baits will hide between rocks or in the weeds if given a chance, a habit that will reduce their visibility to the fish and your likelihood of getting strikes. Corkies and floating jig heads will keep them at the depth you determine by how far up the line your sinker is placed. The best colors for these floats are red, orange, chartreuse and yellow.

46

As the summer progresses and the temperatures rise, the walleyes will go deeper, sometimes as deep as thirty to fifty feet. So must you. The techniques are the same as before but it may be a bit more difficult to locate the right structure.

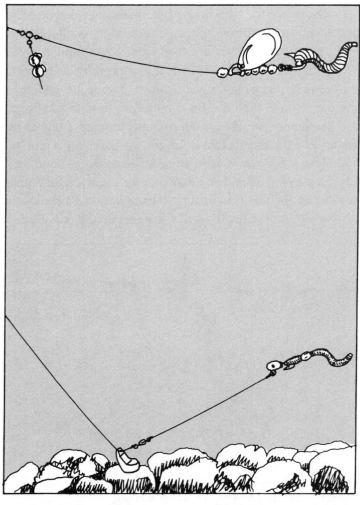

Simple and effective live bait rigs: spinner bladed rig, top, or floating rig to keep bait out of rocks and in the fish's view, bottom.

A good place to start are the same reefs and points you located before. Many of these will run into the deeper water you and the walleyes are seeking.

Evening and morning fishing becomes important during the hotter months because at these times the walleyes will sneak back into the shallower water, thereby giving you easier access to them. The very best time to catch walleyes then will be the first and last hours of light. Night fishing can be very productive as well. This actually works out well for many canoeists as they may wish to travel during the middle of the day or take time out for some other form of recreation.

Remember too, that it doesn't hurt to keep a line in the water as you travel across lakes. By paddling along the shoreline, often necessary anyway because of wind, and dragging a plug behind you may pick up a few fish for dinner. A nice rig for this is a floating Rapala with a sinker of the proper size for the depth fixed a few feet up the line. Besides

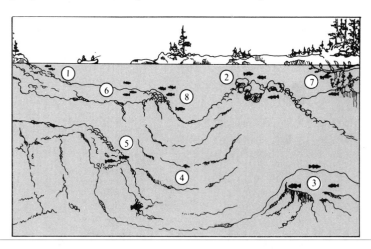

Some typical walleye structures: 1) rocky points; 2) reefs; 3) sunken humps; 4) trenches; 5) the lip or edge of a trench; 6) flat, hardtopped plateaus; 7) weed beds and sunken logs; 8) drop-offs. Generally, the later in the summer, the deeper the fish.

Even rainy days can't dampen the smiles when you catch a nice stringer of walleyes like these.

being a deadly bait, the floating Rapala will rise off the bottom when you stop to check your maps, take a picture or whatever. This will save you a lot of snags and increase your opportunities to catch fish.

Whenever or however you take a walleye in the Canoe Country one thing is for sure, it won't disappoint you when it comes time for a meal. Fresh walleye fillets turning a crispy brown over an open fire is one thing you won't forget when you get back home.

Chapter 4

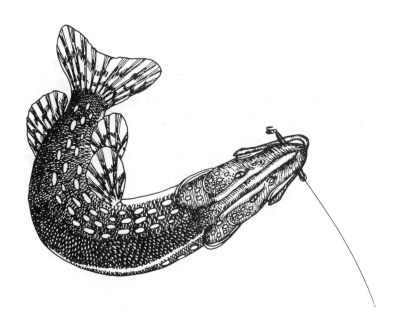

The Northern Pike

I DON'T KNOW how many fishing trips into the wilderness have been rescued or how often the food bag has been stretched by this fish, but I suspect that the Northern Pike has accounted for more of both than can be numbered.

It is not necessary for me to go into how much maligned the Northern Pike is as a game fish. The outdoor magazines tell you about that in every pike story they publish. The fact is that they are first on the list of preferred fish of very few fishermen. Yet, nearly everyone has at least one pike story they tell with much excitement. For, in truth, old *Esox Lucius* is a very exciting fish.

Catching northerns is not hard. They seem to eat just about anything and everything. They probably got their poor reputation because small northerns can sometimes make a nuisance of themselves when you're fishing for some other species. Still, you never hear of anyone being upset over catching a nice one. And most of these are accidents. Catching big northerns consistently is a craft as difficult as any in fishing.

Pike are an efficiently designed eating machine. Their elongated bodies and rear set fins are built for rapid bursts of speed, used to attack their prey. Large, sharp, pointed teeth are made for a quick grab and their smaller, backward slanting teeth in the roof of the mouth are there to insure that their lunch doesn't slip away. Pike make up for any lack of beauty with efficiency and pure savagery.

Northerns are found just about everywhere in the Canoe Country. If a lake has nothing else in it you can bet there are at least a few northerns. And there always seems to be one big one. Northerns have a circumpolar distribution, a range in which the BWCAW and Quetico fall. Though they are not one of this continent's favorite game fish they have long been extremely popular in northland countries worldwide. The fact that they grow even larger in Europe than here may have something to do with it.

The largest northern taken from Minnesota waters is a monster of 45 pounds, 12 ounces. In some good northern lakes the average fish may run near five pounds although the size most of us catch may be more like a couple of pounds.

Northerns live about ten years with a rare fish going on to be twenty years old. Fish older than ten years are the truly large fish. Most northerns mature sexually at three years and the bulk of spawning northerns are less than five years old.

Pike are spring spawners, usually as soon after ice-out as is possible. This occurs in April or May in the Canoe Country, all depending upon the severity of the winter and the warmth

Imagine, if you can, tying into a pike such as this. Big pike lurk in many of the BWCAW's and Quetico's lakes.

of that particular spring. Pike prefer to spawn in shallow, grassy areas, often barely deep enough to cover the adult fish. Although their spawning runs are at night they reserve the actual spawning for daylight hours. The best days for this activity have lots of sun and little wind.

When the pike have finished spawning the fishing is very good. After they move back to their summer haunts they begin to feed heavily. At that time of year the pike are most often found near early weed beds, which generally means they will be in five to eight feet of water over hard soil bottoms. They will cruise the edges of these early weed beds searching for bait fish upon which to prey. If these weeds are near channels between parts of a lake or near shallow drop-offs, so much the better. As during any time of the year, pike like to hang around stumps or fallen trees that are near or within the weed beds. If the weeds haven't sprouted yet, or the lake has few weeds as is the case in many Canoe Country lakes, the northerns will still be found near the channels, drop-offs and stumps, wherever there is sufficient cover to hide the minnows they feed on.

The nice thing about pike is that most of them are caught in less than fifteen feet of water, no matter what time of year. They also respond very well to artificial lures, a happy combination for the wandering canoeist. They like cool water, not cold, and in the Boundary Waters and Quetico they usually don't have much of a problem finding the right temperature without having to go deep. To be sure, some large pike have been taken at great depths, but this is the exception rather than the rule.

Northerns like water less than sixty-five degrees. If the water gets over that temperature the fishing begins to slow down. Since pike will move about though, they will usually not stray too far from their early season haunts, often just sliding out into slightly deeper water in search of the right

When looking for northern pike throughout most of the season, cast toward shore near weed beds and stumpy, brushy areas.

temperature. They commonly move in and out with the rising and setting of the sun. Big northerns will come right up to shore after dark to feed even if the water temperature is considered above their ideal range. Cloudy days with a chop on the water will help keep the shallows a bit cooler and therefore keep the pike shallow as well. When the water temperature gets over sixty-five degrees, and the pike have no access to deeper or cooler water, they will restrict their activity. Only in very shallow lakes will this be a problem.

When looking for pike on spring or early summer trips try first the shallow bays with flat bottoms. These areas warm up a bit sooner and have early weed cover. It is not unusual to take pike in two to five feet of water in these spots at this time of year. By drifting or maneuvering slowly and quietly and casting along weedlines or submerged logs, one should hopefully be able to raise fish. It is important to set the hook hard when you do get a strike as northerns have very bony mouths. As in all fishing, it pays to keep your hooks honed to a razor sharpness.

Use medium to shallow running plugs and spoons when fishing this shallow water. Try to plan your retrieve so that the lure follows the bottom contours rather than running to or away from them. Most of the time it is best to retrieve the lure briskly, fast enough to keep it barely in sight under the water's surface. Because you are fishing in shallow water it pays to keep noise in the canoe to a minimum and the presentation of the bait as quiet as possible.

When the northerns are in the shallows, which can be at nearly any time of the year, surface plugs similar to those used for largemouth bass often work well. The sight of a northern rising to smash a top water lure is one not easily forgotten. These lures are fished much the same way as just described for plugs, spinners and spoons.

Drift silently or anchor and cast the surface plug toward shore. Get it as close to the land as you can. After letting the plug settle down for a minute or so, begin the retrieve. Fish the lure slowly right in the surface film and keep this up until it is right up to the rod. Often a pike will follow the lure for many yards, sizing things up. If the plug is lifted too soon from the water, or you speed up the retrieve because you think it has passed the best cover, the pike may be spooked. Give the fish time. Also, remember there is no such thing as a bad cast. Even if the lure does not land where you had intended, retrieve it with patience. We do not always know where the fish will be nor what is under the water's surface. Fish every cast as though you know there will be a strike. There are also no hard and fast rules to fishing. If the spot looks good and a slow retrieve has produced no strikes, try the same area using a fast retrieve. Pike sometimes strike out of pure orneriness or defensiveness and a quick retrieve can occasionally peak their interest.

Trolling for northerns can be successful, especially when used to do a little fishing while passing through a lake. Troll near weed beds, drop-offs and submerged bars. Go slowly enough that your spoon just wobbles but doesn't spin. If you're using a plug, check its action along the side of the canoe to determine the proper speed, then try to maintain that speed as you paddle along. When pike are shallow, fifty or sixty feet of line is probably enough. Start close to the structure or weed and work your way slightly deeper if need be. You may have to add a small sinker if the fish are down ten or fifteen feet. A keel sinker will help avoid line twist. When you fish deeper it will be necessary to let out a little more line to keep the lure down.

Pike can be taken on a myriad of baits and lures as is evidenced by the accidental catches while fishing for walleye or other fish. They will take anything from the smallest of baits and lures to large plugs, spoons or minnows. Jigs can be very effective on northerns as well. When you're fishing specifically for pike the use of a steel leader, six to ten inches in length, is a must. Their sharp teeth will saw through the heaviest of monofilament line in seconds. Try to avoid the use of these steel leaders, however, when fishing for anything else. They are highly visible to fish and the loss of a few lures to marauding northerns is not worth the diminished catches you will have if they are used while concentrating on any other fish species.

Spoons such as the Daredevle are deadly on northerns. Spoons for pike should be fairly large, between three and five inches in length. Red and white with a silver or copper belly is a standard although silver, hammered brass, blue or black and white have accounted for their share as well. Light colored lures on bright days, dark on dark days, seems to be the rule.

Nearly as effective as spoons are large spinners of the Mepps or Vibrax types. The addition of a buck or squirrel tail to these spinners is a definite advantage as they give the

The pike's tastes are simple. Here are some of the best lures: left to right: Mepps spinner, Lazy Ike, red/white and diamond patterned Daredevles and the versatile Rapala.

lure a touch of color and life. Stick with silver or gold blades and you can't go wrong.

Pike feed mostly on small fish and minnows. Both the spoon and spinner mimic these and that is why they are such good lures for pike. At times equally effective are minnow like plugs such as the Rapala. These are especially productive as a trolling lure although they can be cast into cover if you're using a heavier sinking model or have added weight to the floating ones. A word here about floating versus sinking plugs. Generally, floating models of most plugs have better action than their sinking counterparts. Don't ask me why. Given the choice, I would use a floater with some lead added a few feet up the line rather than the sinking types provided the fishing is done in relatively shallow water. If you are fishing in very deep water, say over fifteen or twenty feet, then you will have to use a sinking model (or add a lot of lead to a floater). The particular advantage to using the floating plug, other than action, is the fact that they hang up less. This is more important while fishing from a canoe than from motorized craft since you are the motor and may need to stop or encounter winds that cause you to slow down. With floating plugs and a sinker the plug will rise off the bottom when you stop or slow down, even if the sinker does touch down. This will greatly reduce the number of snags and lost lures. Plugs for pike are best in silver, gold or perch finishes.

Northerns are not at all bashful about picking up dead bait. It is sometimes impractical to haul quantities of large live bait into the Canoe Country just for pike but frozen, salted or otherwise preserved minnows travel well. For pike, the larger the bait the better. Some optimistic (and knowledge-able) fishermen use sucker minnows large enough to be a good meal for the fisherman as well as the fish. But these large minnows do account for some of the biggest pike caught every year. A minnow harness, available at most bait shops, is used with this large bait in order to insure putting a hook into the fish since a single hook in such a large minnow may miss the fish's jaw when set.

This type of a set up is fished right on the bottom. Large pike don't get that way by turning down a free meal and they often scavenge. When you feel the fish pick up your bait, give him plenty of line. Open the bail of your reel or set it on free spool and let him run until he stops. When the fish begins to move the second time, let him have it. Set the hook hard enough to cross his eyes and then hold on 'cause he's going to be a little angry.

This method of pike fishing works well when the pike have gone a little deeper and is nice on those days when you are feeling just a bit lazy. There really isn't much fisherman

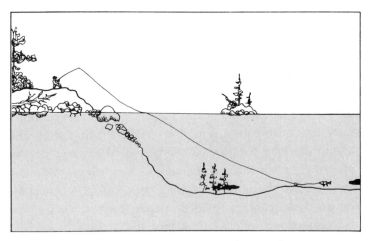

Northerns (and lake trout) often scavenge. A large sucker minnow or smelt fished on the bottom can be effective. The bait need not be live and should be used with a minnow harness to insure hooking the fish.

participation until the battle is on and is a nice way to fish from your campsite. This technique works well on lake trout also.

One of the best times of the year to catch really big pike is in the fall. At this time of year they are feeding heavily before the coming of winter. They move into shallower water and concentrate on schooling minnows. Fish that are normally fussy or cautious lose a considerable amount of their discretion while on these feeding binges. You would fish for these fall pike much as you would in the spring, the fish generally being in the same shallow water. Look for good cover where minnows may hide and that is where the pike will be. At times in the fall, big pike will move onto stormy shores, perhaps to take advantage of the turbid water caused by the waves to ambush their prey. Don't pass these up even though the waves may make the fishing more difficult.

Pike at all times of the year are solitary fish. Unlike other species that are schooling fish and catching one means more, catching more than one pike in a single location is rare unless bait fish are highly concentrated there. That doesn't mean that there may not be more than one pike within casting range. If the habitat is suitable for pike there may well be more than one fish around. They just won't be cozied up to each other like walleyes.

For instance, you will seldom take more than one pike from under the same log or patch of lily pads. They will be somewhat spread around and are territorial by nature. Make sure you cover the area thoroughly before moving on. A big, old pike may be there, just lazily watching your lure go by waiting for something that interests him. Factors such as lure color, size, depth and speed are all in your control. Experiment and be patient, he will probably strike when you've done the right things. In the long run, experimenting with different lures, speeds, etc., will get you more fish more quickly than paddling from one likely looking "hotspot" to the next, wasting valuable fishing time.

At times pike fishing is downright unscientific. Perhaps that is part of its charm. Yet at other times, even northerns can be pretty persnickety. It will be a rare trip into the Canoe Country however, that you can't catch a bunch of northerns for a meal if you want to. If all else fails, and you have a fish dinner on your mind, go catch a pike. Contrary to what some people say about eating northern, I have found them to be excellent from the cold, clean lakes of the north country. When of a decent size, even getting around the oft-cursed "Y" bones is not that hard when filleting. I think you'll find the effort well worth it.

Chapter 5

Canoe Country Lake Trout

PROBABLY NO FISH epitomizes the north country more than the lake trout. *Salvelinus namaycush* is a fish of clean, cold waters. A lake must have plenty of oxygen, even down to its deepest reaches, to be a laker lake. Not a fish to tolerate warm water, lake trout seek out these well oxygenated depths to ride out the hot months. The Canoe Country has plenty of lakes meeting these requirements. It is, in fact, just about the southernmost range in which lake trout are found natively. When you are in lake trout country you know that you are "up north".

Lake trout are one of the main reasons the BWCAW and Quetico are so popular with fishermen. After all, you can catch walleyes, northerns and smallmouth bass elsewhere. But with the exceptions of the Great Lakes, the Northeast and a few scattered areas where they have been introduced, this region contains the most southerly concentration of good lake trout lakes.

Lakers are also a fish made for day-dreaming. They can and do grow to huge size and while these big fish are not the ones that make up the bulk of our catch there is always the chance and hope that we will tie into one. Lake trout well over twenty pounds lurk in the depths of some Canoe Country lakes. It doesn't take too much imagination to picture one of these grey monsters being subdued along side of your canoe.

Many people labor under the common misconception that you can only catch lake trout on light tackle in the spring. Their belief is that during the summer one must use heavy tackle and trolling to take lake trout, both of which are synonymous with work when fishing from a canoe with no motor. This is not strictly true. While spring is the easiest time to catch lakers, you can take them throughout the summer on light tackle with methods we'll get to later in this chapter.

Some of my fondest fishing memories of the Boundary Waters center on spring lake trout trips. Our family traditionally made these early season trips as far back as I can remember, starting with my father who explored these waters back in the late 1940's. One trip in particular sticks out in my mind. It had been a late spring, the kind that make for good lake trout fishing since the surface water remains cold until the season opener. Snow could easily be found on shadowy hillsides and was a great natural refrigerator of lake trout fillets. Poplar trees cast the first faint tinges of new green on the landscape, their small leaves a bright contrast to the deep greens of the pines and spruce. The nights were still chilly enough to freeze the water bottles and make a popsicle of last evening's left over coffee, the kind of nights that, if it wasn't for the thought of those lake trout awaiting, you might never have gotten out of your sleeping bag.

The lake, to remain nameless, couldn't have lost its ice more than a few days before we had arrived. The water was a uniform cold throughout and the lake trout were taking advantage of the warming rays of the sun by feeding heavily along shallow shores and over reefs. A hundred yards or so from the campsite was a reef, marked by what we always referred to as the "sea gull" rock. True to its name there were always sea gulls resting and nesting on the bare protrusion.

This reef is typical of those found in Canoe Country lakes. It began at the rock, dropping down into about ten feet of water rather quickly and gradually got deeper before reaching our island campsite. Along its length you can take lake trout most of the season because it offered the right depth somewhere except, perhaps, during the hottest stretches of the summer.

By taking advantage of the wind and quietly drifting parallel to the reef, casting spoons or bouncing a jig, we took a laker on nearly every cast for the three days we fished. Occasionally, a marauding northern was hooked or sheared off our lures. The fishing was so good that it didn't seem to make much difference what color lure you tossed at them but the fish did show a decided preference to a lure tipped with a small minnow, an occurrence I've found repeated many times with lake trout.

This is spring lake trout fishing at its best. It is one of the fastest types of fishing there is providing you get the right set of conditions. It is important to fish as soon as possible after ice-out, fishing season permitting. At this time of year the water is cold enough for the lake trout to be in what is normally shallow water for them, giving the fisherman a chance to fish them easily on light tackle. The fish move up onto the reefs and shores to take advantage of the better feed and perhaps to find a little warmer water. During a normal spring the warmest water at this time is not too warm for lake trout.

The key water temperature to look for in the spring is forty degrees Fahrenheit. A small pocket thermometer can be helpful in locating water at or about this temperature. Failing to bring a thermometer, try fishing in three to ten feet of water and work deeper if no fish are found. Of course, this advice is of no use if the spring has been early or quickly warms up. I remember one trip where the air temperature shot up to eighty degrees during the first week of fishing season and stayed there the whole time we were out. It quickly drove the fish down and we were lucky to have had along some heavier sinkers in order to reach the fish. Remember that and always throw in some extra heavy sinkers.

The average spring, however, will find the lake trout in shallow water until the first week of June. The earlier you get there the shallower they will be. You should be able to find them on their favorite haunts which, generally speaking, have two points in common. Lake trout like rocks and rubble and rarely are they found in weedy areas or over bare, smooth bottoms.

Lake trout also prefer to have access to deep water and will not be found too far from it. A reef that drops off into the deeps will usually have more fish on it than a reef of the same depth that bottoms out quickly. Large lake trout seem to be found nearer the deep water than will the smaller fish. Look for islands or points that may have rocky reefs extending out into the lake. Shorelines with similar structure running parallel to it are also good locations to try. At this time of year the lakers will seldom be deeper than fifteen feet providing it hasn't been too warm yet. Right after ice-

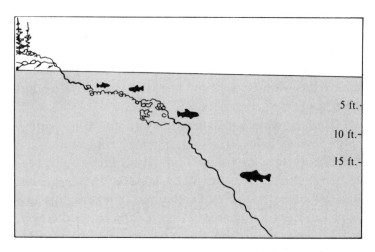

In the spring, lakers are usually quite shallow (5-10 feet), but prefer areas that have access to deep water. Bigger trout are often found closest to deeper water.

out they can be very nearly right up amongst the rocks on shore in only two feet of water! Since they are so light and temperature conscious, try cruising the shallows at dawn and dusk because that will be exactly what the lakers should be doing.

Unless you are adept at recognizing good lake trout waters, a great aid would be a topographic map of your chosen lake or a small fish locator. These will help you locate the reefs and shorelines on which you should be concentrating your efforts. If a map or locator is unavailable, don't despair. Fishermen caught fish for centuries without maps and electronic gear by using their brains and powers of observation. Study the shoreline. A steep cliff along the bank probably means the same is under water, a situation not conducive to good lake trout fishing unless (and rarely) falling rocks have piled up to form a reef. Low, flat areas running down to the shore suggest a bar or reef of similar nature beneath the surface. If the shore of this is composed of rock and rubble,

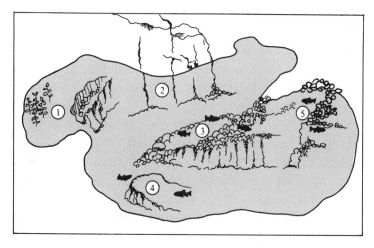

Lake trout are particular. A "typical" trout lake may contain areas like these: 1) shallow, mucky areas with no trout; 2) sheer cliffs dropping rapidly into deep water holding no or few fish; 3) points or reefs that offer a wide range of depths usually hold many fish; 4) sunken reef in deep water with nearly constant depth will have a few fish, perhaps many the peak of summer; 5) rocky shorelines extending out into lake are good particularly in spring.

chances are you've found a good place to start. Those sloping rock shelves so common to these Canadian Shield lakes, the ones as smooth as an elephant's back, seldom belie good fish cover below, no matter what the species you're after. If the trout lake you are on has a stream entering it, especially if it and where it dumps in are rocky, you may have found another hotspot. Water color can tell about what is underneath. Deep water in these lakes tends to be very dark while water over reefs is light, often with a blue-green cast. In short, in the spring you are looking for rocky areas in water anywhere from five to fifteen feet deep. The best spots will have access to deeper water along one or both sides.

Once you have found this type of spot you can work it in a couple of different ways. Probably the best way to ascertain where the fish are is by trolling along or over the spot. This allows you to cover a lot of water relatively quickly until you locate the fish. Once found, you can continue to troll over the fish but your best bet is to anchor, as repeated passes over fish in these clear lakes may tend to spook them. When trolling let out plenty of line, a hundred feet being a minimum. This helps because any fish spooked by your passing will have time to settle down before your lure comes by. Speed is important. Generally speaking, one must troll slowly for lake trout, not perhaps as slow as for walleyes, but still slow. Most people troll too fast. If both you and your partner are paddling very easily, your speed should be about right. Another factor is the type of spoon or plug you are trolling with. Each lure has a speed at which it works best and all in the canoe should have on compatible lures. Try watching your lure alongside the canoe for a few minutes. A spoon should flutter from side to side but never spin. A plug should wobble like the minnow it mimics. Once you have determined the proper speed, let out your line and try to maintain that pace. When fishing deep or with very much line it is OK to pick up the pace slightly.

After locating a good spot, or perhaps after picking up your first lake trout, work the area over methodically. Lakers are not as much of a schooling fish as some but when one is encountered chances are you will find more in close proximity. If your initial technique does not prove successful again, experiment by moving slightly shallower or deeper or by varying lure speed. Prove to yourself that there are no more fish there before moving on. In the long run it will produce more fish than will running all over the lake.

If you have found a "honey hole", your choices of how to fish it are relatively few. Anchoring just off to the side and casting to them with spoons, jigs, plugs or flies is the most productive. This technique spooks the fish the least while keeping you on top of the hole. It is better to work the structure

Their markings and colors make the lake trout one of the Canoe Country's most beautiful fish. This pleased angler holds up a couple of average size lake trout.

by fishing parallel to it rather than toward or away from it. When fishing parallel to a reef you can best control your lure depth, which sometimes is critical. Casting to or away from structure often leaves your lure angling from the right depth. Few strikes will be had if the lure is passing over the fish's head.

Often the canoeist's bane, the wind can also be made to work in your favor when fishing. Suppose you have found a suitable point or reef and have figured out what depth the lakers are at. If there is a breeze blowing in a direction that is parallel or even quartering the structure, you can use it to carry you silently over the fish. In this manner you can either slowly bounce a jig along the bottom and hopefully past fish or you can take casts with spoons and spinners. This allows you to cover more water with a minimum of effort, which is a desirable combination unless you really like to paddle all day.

If the fish are ten or fifteen feet down, you should have no worries about drifting over and spooking them. However, if they are shallower than this try to plan your drift to come alongside where you think the fish are and cast to them. Canoe Country lakes can be extremely clear and the shadow of your canoe passing over may send the fish scurrying to the depths. A slight chop on the water, which is usually the case when drift fishing, will help cut down on this effect.

As mentioned before, be creative. Although lake trout are not the most demanding of fish, you may have to vary your lure speed, color or depth in order to entice repeated strikes. It is far less a waste of time to do this than it is trying to fish the entire lake at one time, especially when you have no motor and crossing these large lakes takes much of your valuable fishing time.

The most consistent lures for spring and early summer fishing are spoons, Mepps type spinners and jigs. Lake trout feed mostly on minnows and bait fish such as ciscoes and whitefish and these lures best imitate them. Spoons are easy to cast in the ½ to ⅞ ounce sizes. The best colors are the old standbys of silver, gold, brass, copper or any combination of these. A dash of fluorescent orange on the spoons can be very effective at times. Jigs are best in white, red/white, yellow, chartreuse and black in sizes ½ and 1 ounce. Your spinners should be in any of the same colors as the spoons and their bucktails should be of the same colors as the jigs. A size three Mepps, give or take a size, is nearly perfect. It almost always seems to produce more strikes if these lures are tipped with a small minnow hooked through the head.

Minnow imitating plugs such as the Rapala and Lazy Ike in bright finishes and colors can be very effective for taking lake trout. These are better suited to trolling as they are a bit more difficult to cast and keep at the right depth than the spoons, spinners and jigs. The countdown models, being somewhat heavier, help in this department. When trolling with plugs, a sinker of the proper size is often needed to get the lure down and should be placed two or three feet up the line. Bead chain sinkers, such as the keel type, will help to avoid line twist.

Some of the most productive spoons over the years have been the Doctor, Sutton, Redeye and the Daredevle in its many variations. The Sutton spoon is not so much designed for casting as it is for trolling. They are sometimes referred to as flutter spoons because of their extreme thinness and light weight. They are popular because their thin profile and light weight give them extremely realistic action.

Another technique, often overlooked, that can be very productive and exciting for taking lake trout is with the use of a flyrod and flies. When the lake trout are up in the shallows there is absolutely no reason a fly can't compete with the

Favorite lake trout lures: (from 12 o'clock, clockwise) Krocodile spoon, Krocodile with hammered finish, two Evil Eyes, Sutton #61, two one ounce jigs, black one has stinger hook, Little Cleo, Red Eye and a Doctor. Center: Heddon Sonar.

other lures. Most people think of fly fishing as dry fly or stream fishing only, including many fly fishermen. Yet, with the use of a large streamer, lake trout can be fished very successfully on a fly rod. Since they are so shallow in the spring a weighted streamer on a floating line is often all that is needed, although I always throw in a sinking tip line just in case. A seven or eight weight rod and line is all that is needed and if you prefer you can even go lighter since you have plenty of room to play the fish. Seven to nine foot tapered leaders with a 3X tippet complete the tackle.

Streamers are the best choice since they imitate minnows. Hook size is not so important as is the length of the dressing on the hook. Brightly dressed flies in gold, grey, silver, red and thousands of combinations and other colors will all work. Hook size need not be large but as a minimum size I would recommend an eight. Sixes and fours would be the norm and are best in a long shank if for no other reason than the ease in tying the fly. Some like to tie in a trailing stinger hook. Traditional patterns are the Grey Ghost, Nine Three, Black Ghost, Black Nose Dace, Royal Coachman and almost any smelt pattern. Muddler minnows, including the variant Marabou muddler, are consistent laker takers. Just about any of these flies and others two or more inches long, snaked amongst the rocks in which the lake trout forage can result in successive strikes. It is pure joy to hook a nice laker on a fly rod and is just about the most fun you can have sitting up in a canoe. A note about fly rod length: the longer the better. Keeping your back cast off the water while sitting in a canoe can be difficult and a long rod will definitely help.

If you are a fly fisherman, don't hesitate to haul your fly rod along if you are planning an ice-out trip for lake trout.

In early to mid-summer lake trout fishing, before the lakes have warmed up too terribly much, fish can usually be found in twenty to fifty feet of water. At these depths, which are not considered extreme for lake trout, you can fish much the same way you would for spring lake trout. The major difference is how much weight you must attach in order to get the lure down to the fish. It also takes a little longer to fish the cover as one must allow for sinking time and longer retrieves.

Start by finding the same or similar reefs you would look for in the spring. Many of these will have deeper stretches along their lengths. If you have a topographic map, find those reefs that would have been too deep during the spring. During this first month of the summer the lake trout should not be extremely deep and may be as shallow as fifteen to twenty feet, especially at dawn and dusk. Once you have located

The lack of a fish locator doesn't mean you can't find hidden structure. By paddling or drifting with the wind and bouncing a heavy jig along the bottom you can find deeper reefs.

a good looking reef or point proceed to fish as described earlier for spring lakers. Locating the fish is the one variable that makes taking lake trout a bit more difficult than in the spring, but once found they will still bite readily.

If you have no map or fish locator and are at a loss as to where to start fishing, a good method is to do a little "sounding" yourself. While drifting or paddling slowly, bounce a fair sized jig along the bottom. By bouncing along in this manner you are sounding the bottom for reefs and drop-offs. At the same time you stand a good chance of hooking a fish. While this method is slow, it is time honored and often overlooked since the invention of fish locators. If you are willing to pack a locator in, it will be a tremendous aid at this time of year.

If you are bottom bouncing, pay close attention to what you are feeling on the end of your line. You want to be aware of changes in the lake's bottom and be able to construct some kind of mental image of what it looks like down there. If you detect an abrupt change in the topography, a few passes should indicate which way the reef runs. Take some bearing from landmarks and start fishing as you would in spring with adjustments in tackle for depth.

Many fishermen who have never fished at these depths before are psychologically put off by it. It is really no more difficult than fishing shallower waters and only requires more lead, time to allow for the lure to sink and paying closer attention to possible strikes. Because of the depth, strikes will feel softer. Monofilament line also will stretch giving a duller sensation. Just keep your line tight and set on any hesitation. Set HARD.

As the summer progresses most people give up on lake trout fishing. The feeling is that since the fish are so deep, anywhere from 35 to 100 feet down, they are impossible to catch. Most believe you must have in your possession deep trolling equipment, that is, wire line, heavy rods and diving planes. The truth be known, even if you did haul all this specialized trolling gear with you it would be extremely difficult to handle without a motor. With all this on the end of your line it would indeed be quite a chore to paddle.

When the lake trout are down at these depths the fishing IS more difficult. But it is not so hard that, if you wish to catch lakers, it is impossible. There are ways, on your summer trips, to catch lake trout that allow you to use the same basic equipment you brought along for the rest of your fishing. While these techniques might work better on equipment specifically designed for them (short, stiff rod and dacron line) the name of the game when you are this far back in the bush is versatility. Your equipment can handle these chores and you can take lake trout from a hundred feet of water. The method is nothing more than vertical jigging, virtually the same technique you would use for ice fishing. The most difficult thing about it is locating the trout. The actual technique is easy.

Summer lake trout are usually below the lake's thermocline. In many lakes there is little or no oxygen below the thermocline but in lake trout lakes these depths have plenty of oxygen. This is what makes them trout lakes. It is at these depths that the lake trout find the temperature they desire, a chill 48° to 54°.

The trick is to locate the fish at these extreme depths. As mentioned before, a topographic map of the lake is a great aid as would be a fish locator. If you have neither of these you can still find these spots by using the "sounding" routine. Remember that, just like in the spring, the good spots are not covering the entire bottom of the lake. It is not a hopeless task even though it is hard to believe when looking at the large expanse of the lake's surface. There will be areas that will highly concentrate the trout due to structure and feed and when found can provide some fantastic fishing.

The best spots will be as near as possible to the early summer reefs, bars, points and the like. If you recall, the best spring reefs were the ones that had access to deep water. Certainly not because the lakers needed the depths at that time of year, but because they move down with the coming of hot weather and warm water. Lake trout are not very migratory in nature and it is a fair bet that they will not have strayed too far.

When doing the bottom bouncing routine go as slowly as possible. Too much slant in your line will mean infrequent or no touch downs with the bottom. Your monofilament line is going to be doing a lot of stretching at these depths so your jigging motions must be greatly exaggerated and done with force to really lift that jig. You can, by the way, do this technique with a spoon if you add plenty of weight. On a dropper from the bottom of a three way swivel, about a foot or more long, attach three to six ounces of lead. At one of the other rings tie in the line from your reel. Then tie on a leader to the opposite end, making it about three feet long. To this apply your chosen spoon (or plug). The dropper with the lead has two advantages over attaching the sinkers directly to your line. First, it allows the lure to rise a couple feet off the bottom making it easier for the fish to see and cutting down on snags. Secondly, if you do hang up, chances are it will be the sinker, not the lure. By using lighter line on the dropper than what is on your reel, or by attaching sinkers that can slide on the line, you will hopefully only break the dropper or slide off the sinkers thereby saving the lure.

Now just paddle slowly or use the wind to take you across your chosen site. Jigs must be jigged viciously about the length of your rod. Spoons can be pumped up and down a bit more leisurely, three to four feet at a time. When you feel a touch down, lift immediately. A strike at these depths will not feel like much, just a heaviness to the line. Often lake trout will grab a lure as it flutters down when you drop the rod tip and when you lift again you will feel a slight hesitation, that heavy feeling. Set the hook and set it HARD!

Once you have found the fish, stay put. If there is no wind you can drift but your best bet is to anchor. You want to be able to jig right on top of the fish. Using $1/2$ to 1 ounce jigs or heavy spoons like the Heddon Sonar or Swedish pimple, continue your jigging. Lift the rod quickly to its full length and then drop it sharply, letting the lure flutter down. Any slight hesitation as you lift may be a fish. Set the hook on all of them and set it hard. It helps to hone your hooks and keep them sharp as all the stretch in your line at these depths will make hooking a bit more difficult. A sharp hook can make all the difference in the world.

The lure colors for deep lake trout are the same as at any other depth with one exception. For some reason, and I don't claim to know why, black jigs work very well. If you are feeling lazy, you can also try sending a preserved smelt

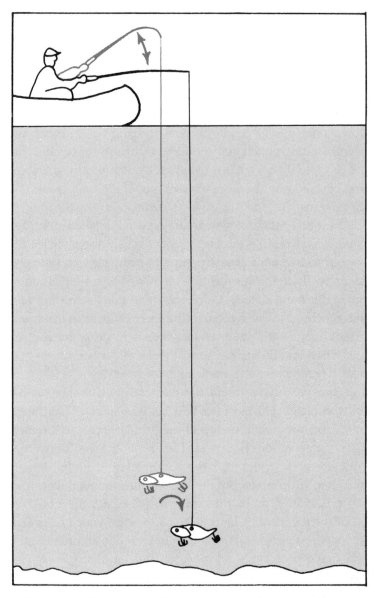

Lake trout can be taken from deep water during the summer by jigging with heavy jigs, Heddon Sonars, Swedish pimples and some spoons. Because monofilament line stretches, jigging motion must be exaggerated, hooks kept sharp to hook fish.

or sucker minnow, six to eight inches long, down to the fish. Lake trout are notorious scavengers and will readily pick up dead bait from the bottom. This is true at any depth or time of year. Try this from your campsite while fixing dinner or on the days that are too windy or miserable to get out and do any serious fishing.

Whether you fish for lake trout shallow or deep they are one fish that should not be passed up. These beautiful wild fish are often highly colored and sometimes look more like their cousin the brook trout. Canoe Country lakers usually have red to salmon colored flesh although some lakes contain fish with a white meat. All are delicious.

The average size is around three pounds but many lakers in the ten to twenty pound class have been taken with a few going even larger. Every trout lake seems to have a different subspecies, with color and size varying widely. It sometimes requires a little creativity with your techniques because in each lake they may behave a bit differently. But with a little luck, some perseverance and these guidelines you should be able to land some of these beautiful fish of the north.

Chapter 6

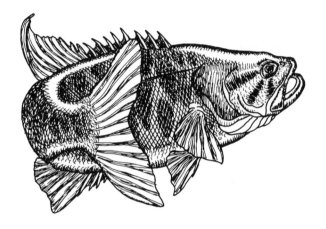

Backwoods Bronzebacks

IT WAS ONE of those incredibly hot and muggy summer days when the effort of any activity would send the stinging sweat running down your forehead and into your eyes. All day long the sun had played hide and seek with ominous black rain clouds, disappearing with the coming of the repetitive and sudden thunder showers. When the sun would reappear, so would the mosquitoes and flies, buzzing lazily toward their victims as if they too were stifled by the heat. Through all of this, with occasional runs to shore when lightning was threatening, we continued to fish for smallmouth.

The weather wasn't what one hopes for on a canoe trip. It also wasn't weather normally conducive to good fishing. Yet after every sudden storm, as the sun came back, so did the smallmouth. Tentatively at first, like the sun, and then aggressively, smashing every bait thrust at them. Most were large fish, running two to three pounds, perhaps recovering more quickly than their little fellows to take advantage of the momentary calm to wolf down some lunch. For this day and the next we caught smallmouth after smallmouth whenever we could venture back onto the lake.

The fishing saved that trip, for despite the weather, which continued to be rotten unless you like being wet, hot and bug bitten all at the same time, we were reluctant to go home and leave the tremendous fishing we were enjoying. And while this kind of weather is not the kind to look for if you're going smallmouth bass fishing, it perhaps teaches us the lesson that nothing about catching fish is a sure bet. If we had paid attention to our natural inclination, which was to curl up and read a book, we would have missed some very good fishing.

I doubt that you could find much more exciting fishing or faster action than tying into a mess of smallmouth bass. This member of the black bass family, with the scientific mouthful name of *Micropterus dolomieui*, provides one of the most exciting fishing opportunities in the Canoe Country.

Although smallmouth are not large in size, the average being one to two pounds, these bronze beauties make up for any lack of size in sheer fighting ability. When I was but a tad of a lad I saw my father battle the first smallmouth I had ever seen. We were fishing one of the big border lakes when he hooked this fish on a yellow hair jig (I remember that well since I insisted he tie an identical jig on my line as soon as he landed the fish) that had been tipped with a minnow. I thought he hooked a tarpon! This fish went crazy, leaping time and time again, each time shaking its head trying to throw that jig. I had only seen that once before, that being in an old movie depicting tarpon fishing, hence my astute identification of his fish. When my dad finally subdued that smallmouth it was obvious to even the untrained eye that this was a big fish. It went over five pounds. My father had caught plenty of fish by this time in his life, though I suspect the numbers of fish went down as the number of children's lines he had to tie, bait and untangle grew, but I still remember his excitement at landing this bass. It wasn't often I saw him get that worked up over something that wasn't my fault.

That's what so fun about smallmouth. Each one, down to those hardly bigger than your lure, is a born battler. For the most part they are also pretty easy to catch, a combination hard to resist. For those who claim they don't like to eat bass, you're in for a big surprise when you sit down to a meal of fresh smallmouth fillets. Taken from the cool waters they love so much, smallmouth are a delight to munch on.

Smallmouth bass really seem to have little in common with their largemouth cousin. Smallmouth much prefer the cool waters of these northwoods lakes and, rather than hiding in the weedy back bays like the largemouth, they are found in clear water over rocky bottoms or in cascading streams. In appearance smallmouth are distinguished by an upper jaw that does not extend back past the eye, as it does on the largemouth. Fin placement and body configuration are nearly identical to the largemouth but smallmouth are usually brown to bronze in color with dark vertical bars, although I have found some lakes in the Quetico-Superior where the bars are nearly indistinguishable and the fish almost a golden hue.

The Canoe Country smallmouth is not native to the area. They were introduced some years ago and have been spreading their range ever since. If there is a waterway connecting two lakes it is only a matter of time and high water until they find their way from one to another. If they find their new home to their liking they will quickly establish themselves. Many former strictly lake trout lakes now have smallmouth populations, to the chagrin of some fishermen and delight of others, since both fish like the cool, clear waters and rubbly bottoms. In most cases they abide together well, the laker using the depths of the lake and the bass the shallows.

Smallmouth are spring spawners, which means, in the Quetico and BWCAW, June. On some cold years you will sometimes catch smallmouth into July that have yet to spawn, their round bellies still swollen with eggs. The depth at which they spawn varies and is determined by water temperature and clarity. They will spawn in water as shallow as a foot or as deep as twenty, wherever they find suitable conditions. The majority of spawning will happen in the shallower end of that range.

The smallmouth's nest is built by the male and they can be extremely territorial at this time. Spawning activities will peak when the water reaches the sixties and if you cruise the shoreline you can often see, with the aid of polarized sunglasses, smallmouth on their spawning beds. These beds appear as a lighter colored dish or bowl, often up to three feet across, on the gravel bottoms.

Usually, smallmouth are found in rocky lakes with a minimum depth of 25 to 30 feet. They like summertime water temperatures of 60 to 80 degrees. Smallies feed mostly on insects and their larvae, crayfish and minnows. Even in the warmest of weather they are almost never found below the thirty foot range and more often than not are found in less than fifteen feet of water. While they can run quite small in some lakes, the Minnesota record is eight pounds. Each year fish close to that record are taken with many four and five pounders being caught. Any smallmouth over a couple of pounds is a handful on light tackle.

The best shorelines for smallmouth are those with rubble bottoms and windfalls that more gradually taper into the depths. The worst are those with smooth shelf rock and/or drop quickly into deep water.

Before the water gets up to seventy degrees the smallmouth will be in eight feet of water or less. They will take surface baits avidly at this time and always prefer small lures or bait. They will also feed voraciously on mayfly hatches. If you are a fly fisherman, never, I repeat, never leave your flyrod at home at anytime of the season if you're headed into smallmouth waters.

When making an early season venture into the Canoe Country, May through the end of June most years, you will find smallmouth in shallow waters. Even though they like cool water, smallmouth will be found in the warmer parts of these cold lakes. This means the shallow shorelines, bays and reefs. Never pass up the chance to fish the mouth of a creek or stream that may be dumping into a bass lake, especially while the water is still cool. These flowing waters wash an abundance of food to the smallmouth and are popular feeding areas even though the lake surrounding the creek's entry point may not appear to be ideal bass cover. Some of the larger streams, if they have good flow and rapids, will

The kind of structure to look for when fishing smallmouth bass: rocky bottoms that drop off to 5 to 15 feet of water.

have smallmouth in them and in this respect they are very trout like.

When trying to decide where to fish for smallmouth, start by looking for shores and points with plenty of rocks and rubble. Not those smooth rock shelves, mind you. They are very poor cover for smallmouth or the critters they feed on. What you are looking for are areas with rocks the size of your fist to the size of your head. If this spot has occasional large boulders dropped there by the untidy receding glaciers, that's OK. Just be sure the bulk of it is made up of the smaller rocks.

Smallmouth hunt in these rocky areas for crayfish, a favorite food, and it provides cover for minnows and insect larvae. All in all, these rubble reefs, shores and points offer the smallmouth a veritable smorgasbord of entrees. You really wouldn't expect them to be anywhere else, would you?

A nice thing about most smallmouth lakes is that because of the water clarity you can often find the right structure just by peering down into the water on the shadowy side of the canoe. Polarized sunglasses are a tremendous aid, allowing you to clearly see the bottom by cutting the glare. At times you will actually see the fish finning lazily along or streaking away.

Smallmouth structure is a lot like that for walleyes in the northwoods lakes. They like drop-offs and at times will suspend off them as would a walleye. They most often congregate on reefs and the like that have a range of depths, so that they can move up or down them according to the water temperature or sunlight. For most of the season you will find them if you seek them in ten to fifteen feet of water.

In the early months shallow bays can often be hotspots. Because they warm more quickly and usually have lush insect and minnow life, they are attractive to smallmouth while the water is still reasonably cool. It pays to check out bays that appear too muddy or weedy for smallmouth, especially if you're having a tough time on the typical structures. Some of these bays may contain a small area of suitable smallmouth habitat and, because of the food and temperature, be a temporary home to them while the water remains cool, often concentrating the bass. Watch for small stretches of rock shoreline or rock piles.

When the bass are in the shallows, perhaps the most exciting way to fish for them is with surface lures and flies. Smallmouth readily take small surface plugs. Even later in the summer they will move back into the shallows at dawn and dusk to take advantage of an insect hatch, again making surface baits ideal.

If you are a spin fisherman, small plugs such as the floating Rapala, Heddon Tiny Torpedo and Jitterbug work very well. Just remember to keep the lure size to about half the size you think it should be. Smallmouth love small baits. The surface plugs for largemouth bass are about two times too big.

Most surface fishing is done along shorelines and the best types for this have a combination of rubble, gradually tapering depth and fallen trees in the water. Once found, approach the area as quietly as possible. If there are two of you fishing it is really much better if you take turns, one person paddling to maintain position. The bow person should swing around to face the stern paddler, in effect making both ends of the canoe a stern end. By doing so, each fisherman has complete control over the canoe when it becomes his time to set down the rod and man the paddle. In this respect the canoe is one of the most versatile of all fishing crafts, quick and easy to maneuver. With just one person at a time fishing, the paddler can quickly back the canoe out of the cover thereby allowing the fishing partner the chance to fight the fish away from obstructions. If you need to scoot in a few yards to make that cast, no sweat. A couple of light paddle strokes from your partner and you're there, with no noise or commotion to spook fish. On calm days with clear water the quiet of a canoe and the low profile it presents to the fish are both big advantages over motorboats. It can make all the difference in your fishing success.

Make your cast as close to shore as is feasible without hanging it in a tree. Let the lure sit quietly on the surface for a minute or so. I really mean a minute, not just a few seconds. Some fish are frightened by the splash down of the plug, others merely intrigued by it. In either case, a wait of a minute will allow them to recover and has been proven, at least to my satisfaction, to increase strikes.

A slow retrieve is in order. As soon as the lure touches the water's surface, pick up the slack and then wait. You want to be ready to set the hook and slack in the line will make this very difficult. Most surface plugs are designed to create a disturbance and gurgling noise. Too fast a retrieve will destroy the intended action of the plug and may turn fish away. You want the plug to sputter and inch along, hoping it appears to the bass as a desirable, but crippled, critter. Plugs like the Rapala, not really intended to be surface plugs, work admirably at this task if you know how to handle them. Cast the Rapala toward shore, as you would any plug, and let it sit. When you begin your retrieve, give it a short jerk and then reel up the slack. The plug will dive a couple of inches and then surface again, the diving lip at its head giving off a sputtering sound as it pulls air down with it. Repeat this sequence all the way back to the canoe. In this manner the Rapala displays the struggling of a wounded minnow and will seldom be passed up once spotted by a bronzeback. When doing any surface fishing, keep the slack out of your line at all times. The sudden swirl of a rising bass can be a shock and you must set hard and instantly. Slack will be your number one nemesis.

When there is an insect hatch on, the surface of the lake can be boiling with rising smallmouth. At these times you can see the rings of the feeding fish or hear the splash of an overly exuberant one. After chasing from one rise to the next, it is my experience that the smallest fish make the most noise, the big ones content to just sip in the bugs.

If you enjoy fly fishing, this is an opportunity hard to pass up. Smallmouth bass are exciting game on a flyrod and respond favorably most of the season since they prefer small baits and never really go deep. If I told you about evenings where just about any fly on every cast resulted in a least a strike, if not a fish on, you may not believe me. But it has happened, and often enough to prove it is not just a chance occurrence. It is at times like this that a fisherman with a flyrod can easily out fish his spinning counterpart, although both will probably catch all the fish they want.

Vertical bars on the smallmouth's side, and its smaller mouth, distinguish it from cousin largemouth. Most smallmouth are a green-gold color.

When fly fishing for smallmouth on the surface just about any surface bug, whether of deer hair or cork, will take fish. Stick to the smaller sizes of traditional bass bugs with sizes six and eight being about right. I have not found the smallmouth to be terribly color conscious but there is some evidence that they prefer light natural colors to bright reds, whites or yellows. It will also pay off to throw in some traditional dry flies in order to match any mayfly hatch you might encounter. These hatches are sporadically spread through the mid part of June into early July. Because the weather this far north can never be counted on, a cold year, or even a cold few weeks, can result in the hatches being delayed until much later than usual. Since flies weigh almost nothing and take little space, it is worth it to throw a few in even if you suspect there may be no hatches at the time of your canoe trip. They will also serve double duty if you decide to stop at one of the stream trout lakes scattered around the Boundary Waters. More on these lakes later.

For fly fishing under the surface throw in some streamer flies such as the muddler minnow, marabou muddler,
eelworm streamers and some minnow imitators like the Mickey
Finn and Coachman. Except when the bass are in very shallow
water or for surface fishing, you will need a sinking tip fly
line. Since smallmouth are in relatively shallow water so much
of the time, you are not at much of a disadvantage using
fly equipment. In fact at times it will be an advantage. Even
when the bass are down fifteen feet, a sink tip fly line will
make fishing this depth easy and successful.

Whether you use flies or lures, make your retrieve all
the way back to the canoe. Bass will come up out of ten
feet of water to take a top water or shallow running lure,
so don't pull it out of the water just because it passed the
shallow area without a strike. It is not uncommon to see two
or three fish following your lure and many times a smallmouth
will follow it quite a distance before deciding to strike. It
is a peculiarity of smallmouth to even observe other fish following a fish you have hooked, running and dodging with
the hooked fish, right up to the canoe.

The fly fisherman would be wise to stick with a seven
weight rod, give or take one line weight, and two lines. A
floating weight forward or bug taper and a sinking tip weight
forward will be all you need. Leaders do not have to be too
long, seven and a half footers work just fine, and should taper
to about a 3X tippet. A few of those ultra tiny split shot tossed
in your kit will be handy to help keep those streamer flies
near the bottom if the need should arise.

The spin fisherman will do well with the basic tackle we
discussed earlier, a medium weight rod and reel. If you are
going in strictly after smallmouth, a light or ultra-light rod
and reel can do the job and will be a ball to use. Your reel
should be filled to the brim with line. By doing so you will
be able to cast a greater distance with ease, an ability that

may be important when the fish are right up on the shoreline, the evening dead calm, and when approaching too near may spook the bass. Six pound test line is more than adequate for smallmouth, or just about anything else, and will cast further and easier than eight or ten pound line.

When the smallmouth are not on the surface or in the shallows along shore, begin your search in slightly deeper water, gradually working your way ten or fifteen feet deep. Stormy weather can put smallmouth down deep, but they will come back up once the weather settles. No matter what the case, stick to the rules and look for those rocky reefs and points. In deep water as well as shallow, smallmouth will be on these types of structures.

Some of the best lures to use when fishing these deeper areas for smallmouth are small spinners. The Mepps and Vibrax spinners are deadly on smallmouth and are especially effective because the spinning blades seem to keep the lure from hanging up in those rock gardens. The best sizes for these spinners are #1 and #2. Black, silver or gold blades will do. I like the ones with the squirrel tails and believe that they are more effective. Besides, they're prettier. Crawl these lures through the rocks with an occasional touchdown and you'll take bass.

I've found that an effective method of fishing a squirrel tail Mepps for smallmouth is to throw them parallel to shore and let them sink to the bottom. A slow, pumping retrieve makes the hair tail flare out, a motion I believe causes the bass to mistake the lure for their favorite food, crayfish. Since the blade revolves in front of the hooks, it acts as a guard, lifting the spinner over obstructions so that, even though you are fishing right on the bottom, snags are not as frequent as you might think. This technique works especially well after the smallmouth have moved into deeper water and by casting parallel to shore, as opposed to casting to shore (shallow

Here are the lures that best take smallmouth bass from the surface to the bottom: (top to bottom) floating plugs, Mepps spinners and rubber bodied jigs.

and retrieving to the canoe (deep water), the spinner will spend more time at the same depth as the fish.

When casting to shore from a canoe, Rapala's Shad Rap is hard to beat. Since this lure dives deeper the faster it is retrieved, reeling faster as the retrieve progresses keeps the lure diving. It helps to hold your rod tip low as well. The key here again is to put, and keep, the lure where the fish are. The perch and crawdad finishes in this lure have turned out to be exceptional smallmouth plugs.

Another favorite smallmouth bass lure is the jig, with the nod going to the rubber bodied kind. Remember to keep the sizes small, the right size for smallmouth being closer to what you would use for panfish than walleye. Most of these lures are available with or without a spinner blade attached above the jig proper. While they are effective without the blade, I believe the flashing blade attracts fish from a greater distance and therefore accounts for more strikes. Any jig for smallmouth bass should be about 1/8 ounce in weight. The best colors are brown, black, purple, yellow and orange. Replacement bodies for these jigs are available and it is a good idea to throw some in your tackle box. A marauding northern can tear these soft rubber bodies to pieces and even the smallmouth are not always easy on them. With a bunch of extra bodies along you'll be able to repair them without having to tie on a whole new lure. You will also be able to change color without going through the whole routine of cutting one off and tying on another.

It often pays to tip your jigs with a piece of nightcrawler or a small leech. For some reason they really like a tipped bait and at times they will take it more readily than the same lure fished without the bait. Perhaps it adds a bit of scent as well as action. Don't gob your worm or leech on the lure. You want it to trail enticingly behind the jig. Hook the leech through the suction cup as you would for still fishing.

This brings us to the subject of live bait fishing for smallmouth. Bronzebacks love leeches and nightcrawlers. At times fishing with these baits can be so fast that you will go through an inordinate amount of bait, especially if there are a lot of small fish where you are fishing.

Use a small bait hook with these baits, about a size six short shank, and a corkie or floating jig head. Corkies are small cork floats, originally developed for steelhead fishing, about the size of a pea or smaller. They are threaded on your line so that they are between the hook and your sinker. In this manner they keep your bait from falling, or crawling, between the rocks, holding them up for the bass to see. Floating jig heads solve the same problem. They look like a standard jig but the bulbous head is made of a floating material instead of lead. Both of these lures work best in bright colors such as orange, pink or chartreuse. At times, when the fish are feeling particularly finicky, a leech or worm on a plain hook or a hook with a small spinner blade just above will do as well or better. The fisherman must impart a little action to these in order to keep them out of the crevices.

All of these should be used in conjunction with a small splitshot sinker, or better yet, a slip sinker. The slip sinker allows the line to run through it and helps to keep the fish from feeling the weight and sensing something isn't what it should be. Sinkers should be placed about eighteen inches above the bait. The slip sinker will require a small swivel tied in at that spot to keep it from sliding to the hook. An $1/8$ ounce sinker is usually enough but if the fish have gone deep or the wind drifts the bait too quickly, a $1/4$ ounce sinker may be needed. This set up can be fished with a bobber and a slip bobber will make it easier to cast when fishing deeper water.

It has been said that one should use dark lures on dark days and light lures on light days. This seems particularly true for smallmouth bass. Some other generalities that hold true for smallmouth include staying away from shores that drop off quickly and fishing shores at dawn and dusk. Shorelines that drop fast into deep water, even if the first few yards appear to be good smallmouth cover, will not be as productive as those shores that more gradually taper out underwater. Everything else being equal, those areas of a lake that have more shallow water, with the correct characteristics, will hold more and larger smallmouth than those areas directly abutting deep water. During the peak of the hot weather period look for smallmouth in water over fifteen feet during the day, shallower at dawn or dusk and on extremely overcast days.

If you remember nothing else from this chapter except that you should use small baits over rocky rubble, you'll take smallmouth. And once you tie into one of these testy little devils you'll always remember just how fun fishing can be.

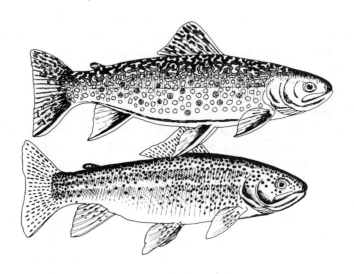

A Mixed Bag

WHILE WALLEYES, northern pike, lake trout and smallmouth bass comprise the bulk of the gamefish species in the Canoe Country, they are by no means the only catchable fish present. Muskies are reported in a couple of lakes, introduced some years ago by man, though their actual presence today may be questionable. Largemouth bass, normally a fish connected with warm southern waters, can be found in a few lakes and provide some very fine fishing. Herring and whitefish, commonly thought of as a commercially harvested species, abide in some of the large walleye and lake trout lakes. When the mayfly hatch is on they are great sport on a flyrod.

Some of the best BWCAW fishing opportunities are those of the stream trout lakes. Lakes, usually small, that the Minnesota DNR deem suitable for trout have been "re-claimed" and stocked with stream trout. These lakes formerly harbored only stunted populations of game fish generally unsuitable for that particular body of water. Many contained no gamefish at all. The DNR, after identifying these lakes, began poisoning them out and stocking them with rainbow trout, brook trout or splake, a cross between lake and brook trout. It has been one of their best programs. Ontario does not have a similar program in the Quetico.

These trout lakes provide a fishery that was otherwise unavailable in this area, with the possible exception of a few lakes and beaver ponds where the brook trout was found naturally. Many of these lakes are not found in the BWCAW but lie around its border. However, there are a few of these little jewels to be found inside the wilderness area and these are listed in this book. If you are passing near one of them it could be worth the detour to give it a try. The reclaimed trout lakes are generally not on heavily used canoe routes and are more often a dead end location. For this reason they are more or less under-fished, although there are a couple that get a fair amount of pressure, especially in winter.

In 1989 the U.S. Forest Service reached an agreement with the Minnesota Department of Natural Resources regarding the continued stocking of stream trout in BWCAW lakes. The introduction of exotic species, fish or wildlife, is not consistent with wilderness management and the agencies decided that there would be no further stocking of fish not native to the watershed, with a few exceptions. This means that splake or brown trout will no longer be stocked within the BWCAW. Rainbow trout, also a non-native to these parts, can be stocked only in lakes that had received them prior to the 1964 wilderness designation or were included into the BWCAW

The secluded waters of the stream trout lakes offer the angler the opportunity for nice brookies like this one.

expansion that came about with the 1978 legislation. That does not mean, though, that just because a lake has previously been stocked with rainbow trout that the MN DNR might not switch it to brook trout for management reasons.

Speaking of which, many of those former splake or rainbow lakes will now be receiving plantings of brook trout, so there should be no net loss in stream trout lakes, just a switch in species. This fish, though not historically found within these particular lakes, is native to the region's watershed and has received approval for further plantings.

If you have never caught a brook trout from these cold northern waters, if you have never seen the jewels on their sides, if you have never tasted one fried to a golden crisp, well then some would say you just haven't lived. Much the same could be said of the rainbow trout in these lakes. While they may be less dramatic in color than cousin brook trout, they make up for it in size and fighting ability, both of which are superior.

These little trout lakes have something special about them besides the fish. With the mist of a cool morning rising from its surface, a more primordial scene could not be found. Even the fact that the very reason you are there is because the lake had been tampered with by man takes away none of its wildness. It just goes to show that sometimes mankind can do things right and actually work with, instead of against, nature.

The wild lakes that comprise the bulk of the stream trout lakes are for the most part lonely bodies of water. Seldom are they the target of the hordes of screaming church and camp groups with their teeming teenagers, a reason in itself to make a side trip.

Because most of these lakes are small, they are also kind of intimate. You'll know what I mean once you've been on one. I can still see the rings of rising trout on the misty calm surface of one such lake. A lone cedar, a pointy silhouette in the morning sun, dipped low over the water as it reached for the far shore. A trout sipped insects from the surface just below the sweep of the tree, comfortable in the tree's shadow. As I watched, my own sips from the steaming coffee cup gradually became gulps, rushing to finish breakfast before the fish quit feeding. Every time a trout rose, I swallowed, the coffee scalding the back of my throat. Soon the entire surface of the little lake was dotted with rings of silently sipping fish. I could stand it no longer and downing the dregs of my coffee, and covering the bowl of flapjack batter, I grabbed my flyrod and slid the canoe quietly into the water, the vision of fresh trout with my soon to be delayed pancakes causing a reaction at the corners of my mouth that would have made Pavlov proud. There are times to eat and there are times to fish, and as it worked out, there are times to eat fish.

When a hatch is on the best way to fish the stream trout lakes is with flies. Fishing to rising trout with hardware or bait is commonly a fruitless experience. They are keyed to insects at this point and the best lure or juiciest worm will seldom draw a strike. The rest of the time, however, both brookies and rainbows will take lures or bait. A word here about bait. There is a restriction on the use of live bait in managed stream trout lakes. You cannot use minnows. Thoughtless anglers have ruined many good lakes by dumping leftover minnows into the water, thereby introducing undesirable species to these carefully balanced ecosystems. So leave the minnows behind. You can use leeches and worms and both of these are effective when fished virtually the same way you would for smallmouth.

The equipment you have with you will suffice for a short stint of fishing in these lakes. The smallest lures in your tackle box will be the ones that will produce the best. Tiny spinners, such as the Mepps and Vibrax, are very good for trout and your smaller plugs and lake trout spoons will produce as well. There are a couple of things that you might want to consider doing that may be different than the rest of your BWCAW fishing. Trout are among the spookiest of fish and a light line is a must. If you have six pound test line on your reel, you can probably get by, but anything heavier will drastically cut down on your fishing success. The best thing to do is carry a spool for your reel containing four pound line or at the very least, tie in a leader of four pound. Carrying a light line like this, whether on a spare reel spool or on a leader wheel, is a good idea for much of your fishing. There are times that even walleyes and smallmouth can be spooky and require that you use light line.

Another hint is that trout seem to like lures that are basically silver or gold. A couple of very good combinations are silver and blue or gold and orange. The silver and gold colors should make up the bulk of the lure's color. A particularly good lure for rainbows in some of these lakes is a small Rapala in silver with a blue back. A spoon I've used with great luck is a gold and orange Krocodile. This one is also a very good spoon for lake trout and splake and is always in my kit.

The one exception to the small lure routine is an abomination called a "cowbell". I first discovered this while my father and I were fishing one of these lakes. We were fishing with more traditional lures, such as already described, and having very poor luck at it. Down the lake a ways was another canoe, heavily laden with three fishermen. We noticed that they were trolling and that their rods were deeply bowed as they bent backwards behind the canoe. They were also consistently catching some very nice rainbows. Not always ready to learn a new technique, I suggested we get closer to the other canoe and see what they were doing. As we slowly, and hopefully nonchalantly, paddled by one of them hooked a fish. When the trout came to boat and was lifted out of the water, we could not believe what we saw. A large string of spinners, easily three feet long with a large blade at the head end and progressively smaller blades toward the lure, dangled ahead of the trout. Attached to the tail end was a small plug, probably a Rapala.

My dad recognized the rig immediately and identified it as a cowbell. It was a lure that he had used out in Lake Superior for lake trout in the '40's and '50's, although a minnow was usually fixed at the end. Needless to say, we were both quite surprised.

Rummaging through his old tackle box, my dad could not find a cowbell. What we did find were a few strip-ons, a long wire with a spinner blade attached, usually used by sliding the wire down the minnow's mouth, out the anus and afixed with a treble hook. By putting a few of these strip-ons together in a row and ending with a Mepps, we came up with something that faintly resembled the cowbell. Lowering them into the water and letting out line, they quickly put a deep bend in our light rods and their thrumming behind the canoe made paddling much work. I wish I could say that we caught a mess of fish but that would be a lie. We did manage to take a couple of fish on this contraption and more importantly, learned that such a thing can work. Am I recommending that you haul one of these things along? Well, for most instances, I wouldn't. But if your sole intention is to fish a rainbow trout lake, it may be worth making room for a cowbell in your kit. My father and I on return trips did catch rainbows on cowbells.

The real trick in catching stream trout in lakes is not so much what they will bite on but where in the devil to find them. Since they are primarily river fish the brookies and rainbows do not seem to relate to lake bottom structure the way other fish do. In fact, they don't pay much attention to it at all. What they are most interested in is the water

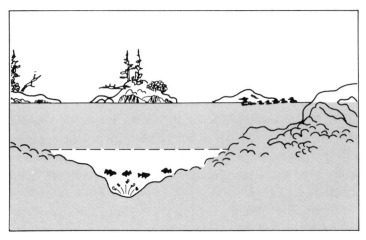

Some stream trout lakes have spring holes that help concentrate trout during summer periods of otherwise warm, low oxygen, water.

temperature, a factor that is critical. Wherever the right temperature is, that is where you will find the fish. It may be on the bottom, close to shore or someplace midway between the surface and the bottom. The second thing that interests them is eating. All trout feed extensively on insects during their early years. As they get larger they eat a lot more minnows and sometimes each other. Big trout are very cannibalistic.

When a combination of temperature and food is right, the fishing will be good. How does one determine this? It takes a lot of trial and error. Again, trolling may be your best bet. By experimenting with location and depth one should be able to catch fish. But unlike other species that are schooling fish, trout in lakes may be scattered over the entire body of water, wherever that temperature coincides with a food source.

In the spring and early summer the trout can and will be scattered in the lakes because the water temperature is often very nearly a constant cool throughout. It does make them a little harder to find but, on the angler's side, almost all of these lakes are small, some even tiny, and it does not take a lot of effort to cover them thoroughly.

Later in the summer, as the waters warm up, the fish can be a bit more concentrated. If you've ever looked at the make-up of some of these lakes you will find that many of them are not very deep. Yet trout must have cool to cold water, their upper temperature range peaking out at a few degrees over seventy. Knowing that the lakes are fairly shallow, and that the DNR wouldn't put trout in lakes that were unsuitable, means that there must be some way of keeping the lakes cold in the summer. I have found that in many cases these lakes are kept cold by springs, often located in the deepest holes in the lake. At times when the rest of the lake has warmed up substantially, the fish really crowd into these spring holes. The result is some very good fishing. Drifting through these holes slowly, using bait, small plugs, hardware or streamers and nymphs is the best way to fish. Keep as quiet as you can. This is true at all times of the year when fishing the stream trout lakes.

Perhaps the most interesting way to fish trout in lakes is by fly fishing. Even when the weather gets hot the trout will move into the shallows at dawn and dusk to take advantage of the insect hatches. If you are a devotee of the fly I would recommend you pack your fly rod when heading into these lakes. The hatches are spread throughout the summer and mirror those of the rest of the Midwest although they are usually a couple of weeks later being this far north. A selection of standard dry flies that work at home will work here and streamers and nymphs produce when the fish are not feeding on the surface.

A floating line for the dries and a sink-tip line for the streamers and nymphs are all that you need. Since even the spring holes in some of the trout lakes are only twenty feet deep a fly fisherman with a sink-tip or sink-head fly line can probe them effectively. Brightly colored streamers and nondescript nymphs should be in your fly box. Try trolling streamers and drifting with nymphs. When trolling for trout with hardware go slowly, slower yet with flies.

Whatever your means of fishing the stream trout lakes, I'm sure you will find it an interesting and rewarding experience.

A few lakes in the Boundary Waters and Quetico contain what are generally considered warm water species and are uncommon to this area, such as panfish and largemouth bass. These lakes are rare and require no special planning. My guess is that if you were really serious about going after these species you could find better lakes to fish than those in the Canoe Country. However, some of the largemouth lakes do have a good fishery and if your itinerary puts you on one of these lakes the techniques that work back home will take them here.

The largemouth I've encountered in this wilderness behave the same as they do elsewhere. They are much fonder of warm water, weedy areas, fallen trees and stumps along shore than are their cousin the smallmouth. They are not fussy about the bottom and you can find them in mucky, warm back bays where no self respecting smallmouth would be caught dead. While they don't reach the size of southern bass, they average a nice size in some lakes and seldom are either overpopulated or stunted. Because the water is cooler than what would be considered ideal largemouth bass temperatures, they never really get to be monsters. The cool, clean waters of the northland make them better eating bass than some I've encountered and they might surprise some who may never have liked bass before.

The equipment that you have for walleye and smallmouth bass fishing will do just fine. Try top water lures along shore or use bait or lures near weedbeds and stumps.

With a little careful planning, some scrutinizing of the information in this book and a willingness to go a bit out of your way, you can end up with a very diversified fishing trip into the Boundary Waters. The really nice thing about this country is that the rewards are seldom not worth the efforts. Even if they don't result in more fish they are bound to leave you with fine memories and scenes of beauty. Fishing trip success is not always measured by the number of dead fish.

Chapter 8

I Caught One – Now What?

CATCHING FISH IS FUN, or at least is supposed to be if you don't take it too seriously. But the enjoyment and responsibility don't end there. All of the fish from the Canoe Country are mighty fine eating if properly cared for between the time they leave the water and enter your mouth. Not every fish that you catch though will share this fate. Some fish will be too small to keep, others may be too big (yes, too big) for your party to consume. On days when the fishing is very good, a limit of fish might be easily obtained and any other fish taken will have to be released to the water. Remember also that because of the cold, long winters and relatively short growing season this far north, large fish take years to get that way and overharvested populations will require years to rebuild. It is your responsibility to kill only what you need for a meal, which is often less than a legal limit, and return all other fish to the lake in as good shape as possible.

In this respect it is the duty of the fisherman to learn the proper handling of fish. It is a terrible waste to get back to camp and find the fish unsuitable to eat. We should also take care while releasing unwanted or not needed fish to insure their best chance of survival. No one will be there to watch you so in all these respects your own conscience must be your guide. It is sometimes a trademark of the species that mankind does not always treat his fellow creatures with the care and respect they deserve. You've gone to the trouble to catch fish, now take the time to release or clean and cook it the right way.

It is a foreign concept to some to throw a fish back, especially a nice size one. In the Canoe Country however, there are no refrigerators or freezers. Most of us will not have a cooler or ice on hand. You will not be able to keep all your fish, not even your limit some days. That doesn't mean you have to stop fishing when you catch enough for a meal. It does mean you need to know how to carefully return that prize to the water.

Two things will be needed to do this effectively. One is a needle nose pliers and the other is wet hands. A lot of folks are afraid of touching fish and swing the fish into the canoe, letting it flop until it is quiet. They then rip the hooks out and flip the fish over the side. I don't know what they are doing fishing or what they could be thinking about, but it certainly isn't the welfare of the fish or the resource. With the wet hands and the pliers you can do it all while the fish is in the water without damaging it.

When you have brought a fish to the side of the canoe and have determined that you want to release it for one reason or another, you must act quickly and calmly. If the fish is hooked in the lips or the jaw, the hook plainly visible, take your needle nose pliers and grasp the hook as close to the point where it enters the flesh as you can. Then simply twist and shake until the hook comes free. All of this should be done while the fish is supported by the water. If you hoist the fish into the air, its own weight will keep the hook from slipping free, not to mention the fact that you may do damage to the internal organs. With lures with more than one set of hooks, be careful of hooking yourself.

If the fish is hooked on the inside of the mouth the process is the same, though a bit more difficult. Hooks that are plainly

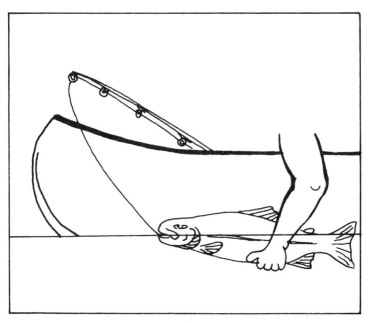

To handle a fish (other than bass which can be lipped) without hurting it, slide **wet** *hand to middle of belly and lift. If a firmer grip is required, grab from top between head and dorsal (top) fin, behind gills, in meaty area.*

visible can be treated like those in the lips or jaw. If they are far enough back to make them hard to get at, you may have to handle the fish. This is where the wet hands come in. All fish secrete a mucous that coats their body and protects them from infections. If this is scraped off, whether by dry hands, dry landing nets or banging around in the canoe, the fish stands a good chance of not surviving once released. A wet hand will affect this mucous much less severely than a dry one. To get at the hook in the mouth, slide your wet hand to the middle of the fish's belly, palm up. You can then lift the fish and turn it so you can see into its mouth to remove the hook. After doing so, release the fish gently. Never toss a fish into the water! Just set it back down. Be careful not to damage the gills by hitting them with the hooks or pliers.

If the fish is very active and squirms around, you may have to apply a little more pressure. Don't do it on the belly but bring your hand up to the back, grasping the fish between the gill covers and the top fin in the firm, meaty area. Try not to stick your fingers in the gills.

Fish hooked in the gills are usually goners. If the fish is hooked lightly and there is no bleeding, you may be able to let it go. Treat it just like you did for a fish hooked in the mouth, taking extra care not to tear the gills. Sometimes the hooks are near the rear of the gills. These are better removed by taking them out through the gill cover opening. Remove the leader or line from the lure and ease the lure

Gripping a smallmouth by its lower lip paralyzes it, allowing you to remove the hook. The bass' small teeth pose no problem.

out, hooks first, through the rear. If the fish bleeds after removal of the hooks, reduce it to your bag. It will not survive.

When using live bait it is not unusual to have a fish swallow the rig, hook, line and sinker as they say. Unless it is easily reached and lightly imbedded you are much better off to simply reach in and snip the line as close to the hook as possible. Don't be lazy or a cheapskate and try to save the hook. A wasted fish just isn't worth a hook. Tests have proven that the fish will survive with the hook left in, especially when the other option is a lot of probing and poking. The fish's own secretions will quickly dissolve the line and eventually the hook.

The key points to remember when releasing a fish are to handle it as little as possible, use wet hands if touching the fish is a must, be careful of the gills and that it is better to leave a hook in than force it out. A fish whose gills are bleeding should not be released.

If you decide to keep the fish you must take care of it as well. A fish that goes belly up alongside the canoe and floats around in the warm water will go bad quickly. Since the canoeing fisherman will seldom have a cooler to put fish in, proper use of a stringer is the only alternative while still on the water.

Whether you use a cord stringer or the type with clips, it is important that it be long enough to allow the fish to get down into cooler water and under the shadow of your canoe. If you can, tie the stringer on the shady side of the canoe. This is more important on hot summer days than those chilly days of spring. The sun can quickly heat up the top layer of water and the additional stress to the fish will cause it to quickly succumb.

Never put the stringer in the fish's mouth and out its gill covering. You are much better off to impale it through one or both lips. If the fish is to be kept alive a long time it should

Except in spring, when water is cool, use stringer long enough to allow fish to reach cooler depth. If possible, keep fish in shade.

be hooked through one lip only. In this manner the fish is free to open its mouth to breathe. Of course, big fish may require that the stringer be placed through both lips so he doesn't twist free. A large fish can put a lot of torque on the clip-on stringers and force the latch open. They have even been known to tear the clip free of the rest of the stringer. It is a matter of judgment whether or not to use both lips. As a general rule, one lip on smaller fish is enough and will keep them alive longer.

When attempting to keep fish alive overnight, add a length of rope to the stringer to allow the fish access to deeper water. The fewer fish per stringer, the longer they will stay alive and the less chance that they will tear free. Keep an eye out for snapping turtles; they have been known to devour fish left on a stringer. There is a much smaller chance of this happening if the fish is still very much alive and alert and the stringer long enough to allow it to keep away from the turtle.

Fish that need to be transported, say across a portage or two, can be kept fresh in an old burlap sack. Leave the fish whole and put them in a completely soaked sack. The evaporation will keep the fish amazingly cool and also prevent flies from doing their thing. Keep it hung up while in camp so air can freely circulate about it, enhancing the evaporation process. Periodically wet down the bag.

Some may question how long a fish will remain fresh enough to be safe to eat. As long as the gills are still red, or pink, the fish should be OK. Once the gills have turned a brown color, chances are you have waited too long before eating it. Another test is to press a finger into a meaty area. If it is very mushy, if your finger leaves an imprint that does not bounce back in a second or two, it may be unsuitable. When the gills still have some color, the flesh still fairly firm and its smell is fresh, go ahead and clean it. It should still make a mighty tasty meal. When it is possible, you are best off to keep the fish alive until it is time to clean it. A sharp rap with a stick or stone behind the eyes on the top of the skull will dispatch it quickly and humanely.

Occasionally we run across a fish that may have a parasite living on them. For the most part this presents no problem and the fish will not only be safe to eat once cooked but also taste just fine.

Parasites may be found on the outside of a fish, in the internal organs or in the flesh. Those found in the internal organs present the smallest problem since these will be discarded with the offal. Try not to puncture the organs while cleaning the fish. Besides allowing parasites to possibly get onto the meat, it just isn't a good practice to allow all that yucky stuff to taint the edible parts.

Parasites on the outside will also not affect the fish's eating quality since most of the time the skin will be removed. While external parasites come in all shapes and types, they are most often found in the gills, eyes or under the scales. Again, they present not much of a problem as these areas will be discarded. One infection that should be avoided are fungal types. Easily recognized, they appear as a white cottony growth of fur or hair on the fish's back, belly and sides. While they are no threat to human safety if the fish is consumed, they impart a bad flavor.

Two other common parasites encountered by fishermen are known as ICH and black spot. ICH is a protozoan that appears as small white spots on the skin or gills. Once the fish is cleaned and skinned it is safe to eat. Black spot is also found on the skin and sometimes in the flesh. These small black cysts look like tiny black spots on the skin or in the flesh. Totally safe to eat once cooked, they impart no bad taste. They rather look like someone heavily peppered the fish while cooking and if you have squeamish members in your party, it is totally allowable to pass it off as such.

One parasite that can be of concern is the broadfish tapeworm. A larval form of tapeworm that can develop into an adult in humans, it is harmful if not killed. They are found most often in northern pike but are not uncommon in walleye, perch and ellpout. Broadfish tapeworms look like a white glistening worm about one to one and a half inches long. It is found in the muscle (flesh) of the fish.

In order to eliminate the danger of introducing this parasite into your own system the fish must be cooked at a temperature of one hundred forty degrees. Unless you consider yourself a campfire gourmet and prepare oriental or South American raw fish cuisine, such as seviche, your normal cooking procedure will render the parasite harmless. Should you be taking fish home with you it is important to know that freezing at zero degrees will also kill it. Cold smoking or pickling without cooking or freezing first may not kill the tapeworm. While not something to cause you to swear off eating fish, there have been a few individuals in this area who have been infected because they did not take the proper precautions.

Just the act of cleaning the fish will eliminate most of your concerns about parasites. More often than not it will be easier to cook the fish and better tasting if it is filleted. By filleting the fish you eliminate the bothersome bones and any "fishy" flavor that some object to. You also leave very little waste and the fillets will cook much more evenly and completely than a fish cut into steaks. The only possible exception to this are small trout which are delicious when cooked whole, sans gills and guts, or boiled fish steaks.

Filleting is not difficult but does require practice and two accessories. One is the fillet knife and the other is a smooth, clean surface upon which to work.

Your fillet knife should be sharp, sharp, sharp! It must have a flexible blade tapering to a fine point of at least six inches. It is awful handy to have some means of sharpening the blade with you on your trip as you should sharpen it about every other fish. Fillet knives are easy to sharpen but for the same reason, dull pretty quickly. You will lend a new definition to the term butchering if you attempt to fillet a fish with a dull knife.

All fish can be filleted and most will be done in the same manner. Northern pike will require a slightly different process to eliminate the "Y" bones that they are noted for. The skin should be removed from all fish although some like to leave the skin on trout. This saves you the messy task of scaling and the skin, especially that of the bass, adds nothing to the flavor and often detracts from it. Lake trout scales are so tiny that if you decide to leave the skin on you'll not need to scale the fish first.

A sharp knife and a smooth work area, such as a canoe paddle, are necessary for filleting.

The other thing you will need to fillet the fish besides the knife is a smooth working area. The bottom of an overturned canoe works nicely as does a canoe paddle blade. Place either of these so that they are level and you are ready to begin.

These instructions are for the right handed individuals. Merely reverse them if you're a lefty.

While everyone probably has a slightly different variation on the process, here is the way I like to fillet fish.

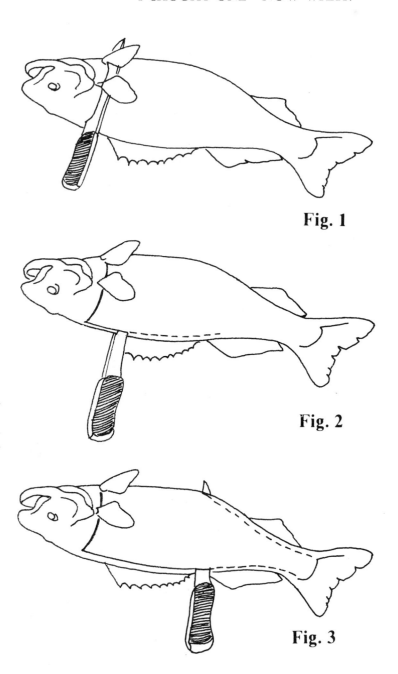

Fig. 1

Fig. 2

Fig. 3

General Filleting

Fig. 1 *Start with the fish on its side, head to your left hand and its back facing you. Make your first cut behind the head and front fin, starting at the back and cutting down toward the belly. This first cut should go only as deep as the spine, which you will feel with the knife blade. Do not cut through the spine.*

Fig. 2 *Now, with the blade turned parallel to the cleaning surface, cut toward the tail. The knife blade should be angled slightly downward to keep it sliding along the spine and the tip of the blade should be tickling the top of the rib cage, which is about half way down the fish's side. Continue cutting toward the tail until you reach the end of the fish's ribs, about two thirds of the way down its length or just in front of where the body begins to taper toward the tail.*

Fig 3. *When you reach this point push the tip of the knife through to the belly...*

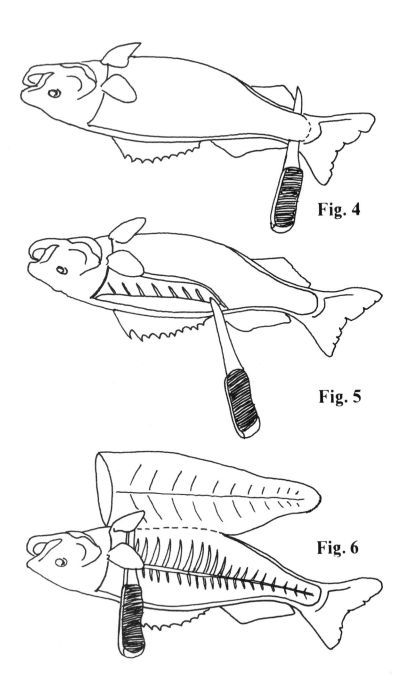

Fig. 4

Fig. 5

Fig. 6

Fig. 4 *...and continue back toward the tail with the blade still sliding along the spine. When you get to the tail, cut through the skin.*

Fig. 5 *The meat is still attached to the ribs at this time so go back up to them. Grab the flesh along the back above where the ribs are and gently lift up, as if you were trying to open a book. While lifting, cut the flesh away from the rib cage with light strokes. This should be done with the tip of the blade and care should be taken not to angle it too much. The meat here is thin and easily cut through or wasted so keep that blade against the rib bones.*

Fig. 6 *Once you have sliced the meat away from the ribs, open the fillet up and slice away at the belly line back toward where you already cut through.*

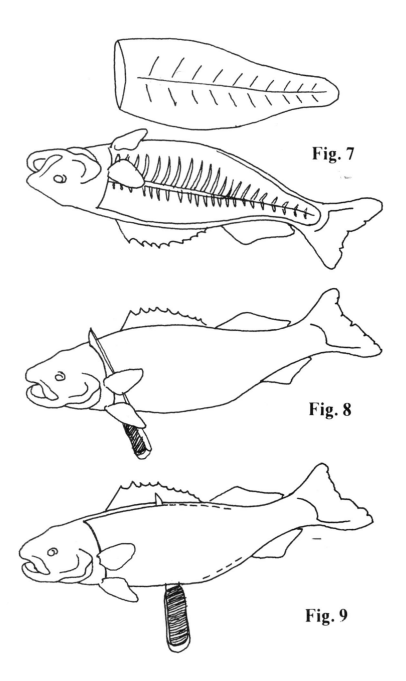

Fig. 7

Fig. 8

Fig. 9

Fig. 7 *You now have one boneless, though unskinned, fillet. Set it aside for now.*

Fig. 8 *Now for side two. Flip the fish over, head still toward your left, and make the same first cut as before, behind the head and front fin stopping at the spine.*

Fig. 9 *Turning the blade edge toward the tail, the knife fully extended from back to belly, cut along the spine back to the tail. This time, you will cut right through the rib cage so you may have to apply a little force.*

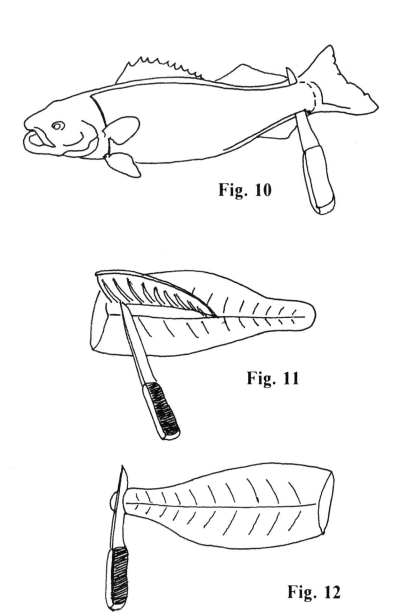

Fig. 10

Fig. 11

Fig. 12

Fig. 10 *After cutting through the ribs continue to the tail and slice through the skin. You will end up with a fillet with the skin and ribs still attached.*

Fig. 11 *Lay the last fillet skin side down with the top of the rib cage toward you. Using the tip of your knife, begin to cut away the ribs at what was the head end. It helps to lift the bones with the fingers of your free hand while sliding the knife between the ribs and the flesh. Again, be careful here as the meat is thin. Because the ribs slant backwards to the tail it is easier to work in that direction. Keep the knife at a slight upward angle. Once done with that you should have two boneless fillets.*

Fig. 12 *All that is left to do is skin the fillets. Starting at the tail, pinch the very tip to the work surface with your fingertips. Take the knife blade and starting as close as you can to your fingertips, cut down ever so slightly until you reach the skin. Be careful not to cut through the skin.*

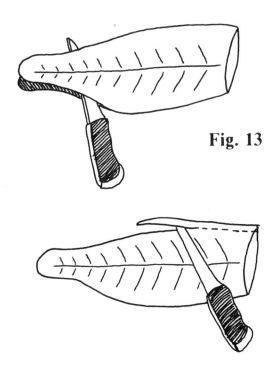

Fig. 13

Fig. 14

Fig. 13 *Now just turn the knife blade flat and slide it up the fillet toward the far end. The blade must be maintained at a very small downward angle so you do not leave any meat attached to the skin. It sometimes helps to use a slight sawing action as you work your way along. This task requires that you use both a little force and at the same time great care. Turn the knife too much one way or the other and you either cut through the skin or the meat. Thin skinned fish like the trout require more caution than do walleyes or bass.*

Fig. 14 *Fillets should be trimmed of belly meat (the white stuff at the bottom that gives off a foul flavor) and any pieces of fins before it is skinned.*

That's about it. You should have two nice boneless fillets all ready for the frying pan. At this point they should be rinsed off and cut into smaller pieces for cooking, if needed.

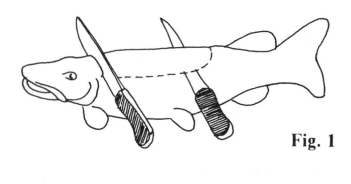

Fig. 1

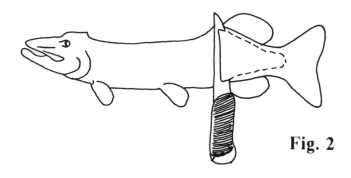

Fig. 2

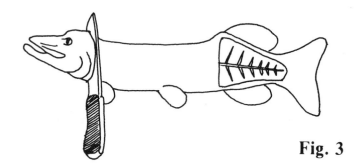

Fig. 3

If you are lucky enough to land a big northern pike and have a hankering for a fish dinner, you should find it suitable dinner fare. One can still fillet pike, regardless of the "Y" bones that inhabit the fleshy sides, and end up with boneless portions. It requires that you modify the procedure just outlined. Let's go through it step by step.

Northern Pike Filleting

Fig. 1 *To fillet a northern pike, first lay it on its belly, not its side. If you are right handed its head should face toward your left. Hold it by the head and make your first cut just behind it down until you hit the spine. Do not cut through the spine. Now turn the blade toward the tail and slide it along the backbone until you get to the back (dorsal) fin which is set far back on a pike's body. At that point cut upwards and remove the first fillet.*

Fig. 2 *Turn the fish on its side now and look toward the tail. Just below the point where you ended the top cut is where you will make the next incision. This area of a pike does not contain "Y" bones so its removal is straightforward and similar to what we've discussed for other fish. Cut down to the backbone at a point just in front of the dorsal fin. When you reach the spine, do not cut through but turn the blade toward the tail. Slide the knife along the spine and slice through the skin at the tail just like you would for any species. Flip the fish over and do this same step on the other side. You should now have three fillets.*

Fig. 3 *Now for the fun part. On both sides of the fish make a cut just behind the head stopping at the backbone, just as you did in step one for the other species.*

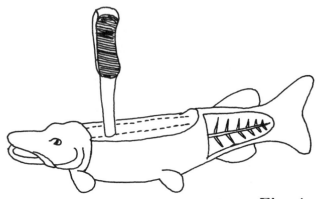

Fig. 4

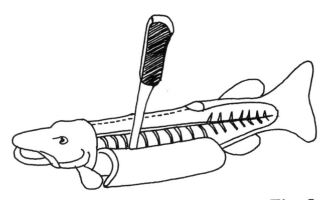

Fig. 5

Fig. 4 *Now put the pike back up on its belly. Looking down you should see the spine and a row of small bones running parallel on either side. If you can't see them, run your fingertip along the flesh and you will feel them. Take the very tip of your knife and insert it on the outside of one of these rows. Cut along this row back toward the tail with the tip of the knife angling slightly toward the center of the fish. Remember, these bones are not called "Y" bones for nothing. You are trying to run the knife along the outside edge of one of the arms of the "Y" while at the same time while working to the tail.*

Fig. 5 *After you've cut a little way down toward the belly you can gently begin to peel the flesh away while cutting. Soon you will reach the outside of the ribs. Using your knife tip follow the ribs down toward the belly and back toward the tail. When you've reached both the bottom and the back edge of the ribs you can cut the fillet away from the carcass. Repeat this procedure on the other side and you should end up with a total of five fillets.*

These can then be skinned as you would any fillet although that top cut fillet may be a bit difficult because of its rounded shape. By following the knife blade closely with your hand and forcing the skin flat as you separate it from the flesh (the fish's, not your hand's) you should be able to remove the skin in one piece. If you have problems with this step, first swear (it helps relieve tension) then scale this piece and cook with the skin on.

With a little practice and some patience you should be able to master these techniques. Filleted fish are much better eating, quicker cooking and less of a mess than fish merely gutted, gilled and steaked.

Now that you're done cleaning the fish, and before you sit down to enjoy the fine meal those fillets will make, you are faced with the task of properly disposing of the carcass and entrails.

Don't throw them in the water off your campsite. Believe me, the minnows won't "clean it up" nor will the turtles. Most of the time it will lay there on the bottom looking back up at you and every other camper who comes along for many weeks. The best thing to do with fish remains is to place them on a rock near the water's edge, well away from camp. More often than not, gulls will devour them in no time at all. If they, or other scavengers, haven't made a meal of the carcass before you leave your site, take the carcass back into the woods and bury in a shallow hole and do this far away from camp.

Fishermen often get labeled as slobs. When other wilderness users find a rotting walleye carcass in their drinking water in front of camp, you can hardly blame them for making that accusation. Take care to leave your campsite clean and free of such things as fish remains, shoreline rocks covered with dried blood and scales (rinse them down when you're done cleaning fish), lure packages and coils of used monofilament. Like practicing catch and release, such "no-trace" camping techniques prove that you really are concerned about our natural resources and leave you feeling good.

Few meals are as enjoyable as those cooked out of doors, whether over an open fire or atop your camp stove. We've all heard the adage that anything cooked and eaten outside tastes better. This is especially true when it comes to fish since it gives you the opportunity to eat truly fresh fish. Eaten

A meal worth working for; crisp, golden fillets so fresh they flip themselves over.

"right off the hook" is about as fresh as you can get.

When cooking fish, either in the field or at home, it is important to remember not to overcook it. Fish loses much of its flavor, most of its moisture and nearly all of its nutritional value when overdone. There are no hard and fast rules as to how to tell when a fish is done, particularly when it has been filleted since one of the most common tests is to pull out a bone and see if the flesh sticks to it. Once filleted you should have no bones in your fish. Another rule says to cook until flaky (the fish, not the cook) but this often results in fish too well done, especially if the fish being prepared is one of the drier species which includes bass, walleye and specifically northern pike which is one of the driest of fresh water fish. Lake trout, because of its rich, oily texture can stand this test. Only time and experience can make the cook a good judge in this respect.

For your camp cooking of fish not many accessories or condiments will be needed. A frying pan or skillet is a must and a spatula will make the task easier. Those tiny frying pans that come with commercial camp cook kits are practically useless. Better yet are aluminum fry pans of at least a nine or ten inch diameter. These are available with fold down handles for camping (expensive) or one can purchase nearly the same pan at most hardware or department stores with a fixed handle (about half the price). Detach the fixed handle and get a pot lifter from a camping supply store. It's nice if they are coated with a non-stick surface to make your clean-up time shorter. Skillets, the flat rectangular kind with a non-stick surface, are extremely handy when cooking for a larger party because of their big size. Foods in the out of doors cool quickly and it is nice to be able to cook enough for all at the same time, the skillet allowing you to cook two foods or plenty of fish for all and eliminate the eating in shifts syndrome. You may need two cook stoves under the skillet to heat its entire surface evenly. A nice light plastic spatula will allow you to turn those fillets without crumbling.

You'll probably need some oil or margarine to cook the fish in. The oil transports better and keeps longer than either butter or margarine. Pick up a small plastic bottle from a backpacking shop so you don't have it leaking on your sleeping bag in the pack. Salt and pepper, as well as any other spices your little heart desires should be taken along on the trip. They are light and use up little space besides adding something special to your camp cuisine. A nice container for storing spices are those little plastic canisters that 35mm film is packaged in. Snap on lids with shaker tops are available from outfitters and mail order houses to make these canisters perfect for camping.

About the only other supplies you need for cooking fish in camp are flour, cornmeal or cornflake crumbs. You need not bring all of these, just your favorite. Each is used for coating the fillets, all are good, and which one to use is strictly a matter of personal preference.

Most recipes will call for filleted fish but there are a couple of instances where whole or steaked fish may be used. Try to keep your camp cooking as simple as possible. The fresh fish won't need fancy recipes or much dressing up to make them delicious.

If you spend a bit of time on a stream trout lake you may have caught a few pan sized trout. Not many fish can compare to the delicate flavor of trout when cooked to a golden crisp. Here is a time honored way to cook small trout:

- salt and pepper
- fresh trout, gutted and gilled but with head and tail left on
- some flour, cornmeal or cornflake crumbs
- butter or oil

Simply salt, pepper and then coat the trout by rolling them in your choice of coating mix. Put the butter or oil in a pan that is over a medium heat. Low to medium heat will allow you to cook the trout slowly and brown it as well. Depending on the size of the fish the entire cooking time will run about 15-20 minutes.

Once the coating mix has set on one side, flip the trout over gently. Brown the other side. Make sure it doesn't burn to the pan. It will require about 10 minutes of slow cooking on each side to brown them to perfection.

When they are thoroughly browned, serve. Be careful not to break the fish into chunks. To eat, just remove the small fins about the fish with a light tug. Leave the head and tail on to serve as handles and eat right off the bones, corn on the cob style.

Another method of preparing small trout whole, sans gills and guts, is wrapped in tinfoil and place under coals. If you are one of those who carries fresh veggies on your canoe trips, dice up some carrots, onion, celery or what have you and stuff the fish after sprinkling them inside and out with salt and pepper. Wrap each one in a piece of foil and bake under coals for 15-20 minutes. The U.S. Forest Service campfire grates are a hindrance here but if you clean out the mess left by previous campers you should have room to work under them. Don't build a fire outside of the designated spot. By the way, you can prepare the fish this way without vegetables.

About the only justifiable reason for preparing fish in a steaked form (cleaned and cut into 1-2 inch wide slices from back to belly) is when used as poor man's lobster. Lake trout lend themselves particularly well to this method of cooking. Because lake trout are an oily fish, this method renders them especially tasty as the oil is boiled away. You'll need a couple of things special for this recipe so if you plan a lake trout trip, make provisions for hauling them along. It's a simple method of cooking fish and here is what you'll need:

- lake trout, steaked (skin on)
- salt, about a palm full
- a bay leaf or two
- a half dozen peppercorns
- butter or margarine (preferably butter)
- a dash of lemon juice (optional)
- a hunk of cheesecloth (optional)

Bring water to boil in as big a pot as you have. Throw in the salt, bay leaf and peppercorns. Sit back and swat flies for a few minutes until this comes back to a boil and stews for about five minutes. If you have cheesecloth, wrap the trout steaks in it and lower into the water. You do not need the cheesecloth but it will help to keep the steaks in one piece. If you have none, just be careful when removing the steaks. Continue to boil for about five to seven minutes or until the fish starts to turn white. While doing this step melt some butter or margarine in a pan and when melted, stir in lemon juice, if available. Remove the fish when done, discard the skin and dip the chunks into the butter as you would lobster. Enjoy. If the fish is done properly, it will fall easily off the bones. Contrary to old wive's tales, I've found that mature lake trout have better flavor than young ones, though they are oilier. This method is particularly nice for those big, old fish.

I suspect that most of the time your fish dinner will be simply fried. Fine. It's hard to beat a shore lunch of golden, crispy fillets fried just so. All fish can be prepared this way but are slightly different in their requirements. For instance, you can leave the skin on trout but it should be removed on most other species. This is a must for bass whether large-mouth or smallmouth. Bass improve dramatically in palatability when the skin is discarded before cooking and can compare favorably with walleye if this step is performed. Northern pike require less cooking time, or a lower temperature so they do not dry out, though thorough cooking of pike is important to safeguard against tapeworm contamination. Lake trout should cook a bit longer because of their oil content. To prepare any fish by frying, you'll need the following:

- fillets, rinsed and left damp
- salt, pepper or your choice of seasonings
- cornmeal, flour or cornflake crumbs
- butter, margarine or oil

Bring the butter, margarine or oil to a hot, but not smoking, temperature. The deeper the fat, the more the fish will be deep fried. To simply fry, you'll want about a quarter of an inch of fat in the bottom of the pan. To deep fry, it should nearly, if not completely, cover the fillet. If your choice of grease is too hot you will end up with fish that is crisp on the outside, if not burned, and under done in the center. Practice will make perfect.

Take the damp fillets and dip them in your choice of coating mix. If you have a bag with you, putting the mix and fish in the bag and shaking will provide a more even coating. The salt and pepper can either be shook into the coating mix before applying the fish or sprinkled directly on the uncoated fillets. Now, just drop the prepared fillets into the hot fat and fry. When the coating has set up on one side, a matter of a few seconds, flip it over. Total cooking time for both sides will be somewhat less than ten minutes unless the fillets are over an inch thick. Thin fillets cook more quickly and generally taste better than thick ones. If the fish you filleted is a large one, and the fillets thick, you might want to consider slicing them lengthwise into thinner pieces.

When the fillets have turned a crisp brown, serve. Keep an eye on your party member who is wolfing his serving down. Chances are he has his eye on not only his second piece but yours as well. You must be assertive here. Place yourself between him and the frying pan, even eat standing if you must. These degenerate fillet thieves deserve no quarter.

Simple things, well earned, are the best things in life. Your own effort put you into this wonderful back country and supplied you with dinner. Done properly, fresh fish dinners will not only be something fondly remembered once home again, but greatly anticipated when planning your next trip. By taking care of fish from the time they are landed, whether released or saved for dinner, you can insure better fishing years down the road or some mighty fine eating back at camp. It brings the whole experience full circle.

Chapter 9

A Lake Index
and How to Use It

ONE OF THE GREATEST pleasures of the Canoe
Country is the sense of personal exploration involved. Around
every bend, at the end of each portage, are new panoramas
and waters to be discovered. For some it is enough just to
see and experience. For me, well, seeing new things just leads
to new questions. A perpetual dreamer, I conjure up visions
of large northerns under each lily pad I pass or big lake trout
lurking in the lake's dark fathoms.

I want to know more about each lake, not to the point
where no mystery remains but enough to get me started on
finding a campsite or catching a few fish for dinner. While
leaving some things to your imagination is good for you, fishing
a lake that you know nothing about can be very hard on
your frustration threshold.

I know I'm not the only one who wants to visit new waters
but, because of time or the surety of a successful trip, keep
returning to familiar haunts. Visiting lakes that are familiar

and sure bets is like stopping by to chat with an old friend. It's comfortable. But even the dearest of friends can get to be a bore. In order to change this pattern it helps to have enough information to get you started in the new direction. What you really need to know are the basics. Is the lake large, deep? Can you camp there? Is it accessible? What kind of fish are in it? Is it heavily fished?

Hopefully this index will answer those questions for you most of the time. Since there was no one single source for this information before this book, it was sometimes difficult to obtain. Part of the answers were in the Minnesota Department of Natural Resources files. Some were in the U.S. Forest Service's. The Ontario Ministry of Natural Resources provided what information they had available on lakes within Quetico Provincial Park.

Compiling this information I found that much of it was scattered or incomplete. Cross indexing the files of the various agencies helped to fill in some gaps, talking to locals (those who were willing) filled in others. The personnel of those state, provincial and federal agencies were extremely helpful in adding facts that had not yet reached their files or were currently unavailable to the general public. Without their cooperation the information in this index could not have been gathered.

Still, I am sure, you will run across instances where the information is not complete. You should, however, find the data presented accurate and up to date. Some lakes have been omitted on purpose for a variety of reasons. For the most part they were extremely small and with no access. Other lakes were included where the information is not complete because I felt that the information that was available (perhaps there is a campsite on the lake) is important. Nearly every lake over the size of some malaria infested swamp hole has been included, counting a few that fit that description.

A LAKE INDEX AND HOW TO USE IT

The lakes are listed alphabetically. To narrow things down, the county in which BWCAW lakes are found is also given. For those not overly familiar with the region, the three counties in which the BWCAW falls are St. Louis, Lake and Cook with them running west to east respectively.

BWCAW lake location is represented by township and range. This is not a complete description but will indicate where the lake is. These coordinates can be found on county maps, some of the commercial BWCAW maps and the USFS's Superior National Forest map. I suggest obtaining the last map as a guide to use with this index and for determining which U.S. Geological Survey or Boundary Waters maps to purchase for use on your trip. You can obtain the Forest Service map by writing to the Forest Supervisor, P.O. Box 338, Duluth, MN 55801 or you can pick one up at any Superior National Forest Office. This large scale map (^{1}/4' to the mile) is available for two dollars.

Information on Quetico lakes is scant. Ministry of Natural Resources files locate the lakes by longitude and latitude. The majority of Quetico visitors, however, use either the Fisher or McKenzie canoe maps or the excellent map published by the Quetico Foundation (which can be obtained for $9.00 Canadian from Quetico Provincial Park officials). No coordinates are found on any of these maps that relate to the Ministry's files. I therefore have listed the Quetico lakes only alphabetically and give both acreage and fish species present. Since few of these lakes have ever been surveyed completely, you will not find the depth or littoral percent listed. Because you may camp anywhere you wish in the Quetico, campsite information is redundant. Suffice it to say that it will be a rare lake that does not have a suitable campsite along its piney shores.

Canoe maps are available from two sources. For more information on these maps write to McKenzie Products, 315

West Michigan Street, Duluth, MN 55802 or W.A. Fisher Company, Box 1107, Virginia, MN 55792.

U.S. Geological Quadrangle maps can be purchased from the Denver Distribution Center, U.S. Geological Survey, Denver Federal Center, Building 41, Denver, Colorado 80225. If you are unsure of which maps to order, ask for their Minnesota quadrangle index.

I've included the names of the USFS District and DNR Fisheries Office under whose supervision BWCAW lands and waters fall. You can write or call these area offices for further information. The USFS District offices can tell you more about access, permits, fire conditions and the trails. Check with the DNR if you desire more specific information about the fisheries. The addresses for these offices are found in the last chapter of this book, as is the Quetico information.

Fishing pressure (FP), when available, has been listed. It is based on DNR appraisals that are used statewide and is open to interpretation. Obviously, few of the lakes in the BWCAW are as heavily fished as those closer to metropolitan centers or those open to the use of outboard motors. When used to interpret the actual pressure on the fisheries in a given lake, these estimates are likely to be quite accurate. But a lake in the Boundary Waters that receives even moderate pressure may have too many people on it for those who desire solitude. Those lakes that have no fishing pressure listed are those where it was an unknown quantity and therefore is probably pretty light.

Wherever there is a blank in a column it is because the information is unknown officially. A blank is not the same as a "no" or "none". If a no is under the access or fish column it is because there is no maintained access or there really are no fish, as in a lake that dies out in the winter.

Lake size is measured in acres. Lake size can be an important consideration since both canoeing and fishing can be more difficult on very big water.

BWCAW lake access is denominated by a code. This will tell you whether the lake is reachable by portage or trail, has a boat landing or by a connecting waterway. If there is an "x" in this column, designated campsites are available. Be cautious here. From time to time the Forest Service closes or moves a campsite due to overuse. While this listing is as up to date as possible, time can change this. A double "x" denotes a campground, such as those accessible to cars and are usually found on lakes on the periphery of the BWCAW.

Both the littoral acres by percent and the maximum depth are shown for Boundary Waters lakes. The littoral acres by percent refers to the percentage of the lake that is less than fifteen feet deep. It can be helpful in determining where the fish may be, how warm the water is likely to get and what the water quality (for drinking) might be like when the weather gets hot. The maximum depth is fairly self explanatory. Use it by comparing it with the littoral percent to gain a general idea of how deep the lake is throughout, how cold it is, etc.

Last but not least is the list for each type of game fish in the lake. To the best of my knowledge this information is accurate and up to date. The order in which the fish are listed in no way indicates any preference or numbers present.

A LAKE INDEX AND HOW TO USE IT

KEY

County
- **StL** -St. Louis
- **L** -Lake
- **C** -Cook

USFS District Offices
- **G** -Gunflint
- **I** -Isabella
- **K** -Kawishiwi
- **L** -La Croix
- **T** -Tote

MN DNR Fisheries Offices
- **E** -Ely
- **F** -Finland
- **I** -International Falls
- **GM** -Grand Marais

Fishing pressure
- **L** -Light
- **M** -Moderate
- **H** -Heavy

Access
- **P** -Maintained portage or trail
- **BI** -Boat landing
- **CW** -Connecting waterway
- **x** -designated USFS campsites (must have USFS firegrate & latrine)
- **xx** -Forest Service campground

Littoral acres by percent - L

Maximum lake depth - D

Fish species

NP -Northern pike		**W** -Walleye
T -Lake trout		**SB** -Smallmouth bass
LB -Largemouth bass		**Big** -Bluegill
Sf -Sunfish		**Cr** -Crappie
Rb -Rock bass		**Bt** -Brook trout
Rt -Rainbow trout		**Sp** -Splake
Msk -Muskie		**Stg** -Sturgeon
Pch -Perch		

BWCAW LAKE INDEX

Lake Name	County	USFS Dist.	DNR Off.	Loc.	FP	Acc.	Acres	L	D	Fish
ABINODJI	L	K	E	64-8	L	Px	39	55	33	NP
ABITA	C	G	GM	63-1	L	P	102	100	14	Pch
ADA	C	T	GM	63-4	M	Px	28	100	13	NP
ADAMS	L	T	E	64-6	L	Px	590	26	84	NP, W, Sf, T
ADVENTURE	L	K	E	64-8	L	No	51	100	9	NP, W
AFTON	L	B	GM	64-5	L	Px	50			NP
AGAMOK	L	G	E	64-5	L	Px	113	75	29	
AGAWATO	StL	L	E	66-14	L	Px	39	40	58	NP
AGNES	StL	L	E	66-13	L	Px	1,069	46	30	W, SB, NP, Sa
AHMAKOSE	L	K	E	64-7	L	P	49	21	75	T
AHSUB	L	K	E	64-8	L	Px	70	38	78	Bt
ALDER	C	G	GM	64-1	L	Px	342	27	72	T, W, NP, SB
ALICE	L	K	E	63-7	L	Px	1,684	21	53	W, NP, Blg
ALLEN	C	G	GM	64-2		Px	52			NP
ALPINE	C	G	GM	65-5	L	Px	999	48	65	T, NP, W, SB
ALRUSS	StL	K	E	64-11		P	30	47	45	Bt, Rt
ALSIKE	L	I	F	60-10			30	97	16	None
ALTON	C	T	F	62-4,5	M	Px	1,076	31	72	T, NP, W, SB
ALWORTH	L	K	E	54-7	L	Px	228	38	33	W,NP
AMBER	L	T	E	63-7	L	Px	157	55	27	W.NP
AMINI	L	T	E	64-6		Px	23			

Lake Name	County	USFS Dist.	DNR Off.	Loc.	FP	Acc.	Acres	L	D	Fish
AMOEBER	L	K	E	65-6	L	P x	541	28	110	T, W, NP
ANGLEWORM	StL	K	E	65-12	L	P x	148	100	11	W,NP
ANIT	L	T	E	64-6	L		20	73	19	NP
ANNIE	L	K	E	65-6	L	P	23	91	16	NP
ARCH	StL	L	E	67-14		P x	49			
ARKOSE	L	K	E	64-7	L	No	22	31	37	Sf
ARROW (North)	L	K	F	62-7	L		13			NP
ARROW (Middle)	L	I	F	62-7	L	P	33	100	6	NP
ARROW (South)	L	I	F	62-7	L	P	25	100	12	NP
ASHDICK	L	K	E	66-6	L	P	122	63	50	NP, LB
ASHIGAN	L	K	E	64-8	L	P x	163	5	59	SB, Sf
BAKER	C	T	GM	62-4	L	Bl xx	22	100	8	NP, Pch
BALD EAGLE	L	K	E	61-10 62-9,10	L	P x	1.507	75	36	W, NP, Cr
BANADAD	C	G	GM	64-2	L	P x	211		48	NP
BANDANA	L	I	F	60-9	L	No	10		20	W, NP, Cr
BARTER	L	K	E	65-6	L	P x	11	100	8	NP
BARTO	C	T	F	63-5	L	P x	125	97	40	Sf
BASKATONG	L	T	F	62-6	L	P x	81	100	6	NP
BASSWOOD	L	K	E	64-9	L	P x	14,610		111	W, SB, T, NP
BAT	C	G	GM	64-5	L	P x	91	24	110	T

Lake Name	County	USFS Dist.	DNR Off.	Loc.	FP	Acc.	Acres	L	D	Fish
BATISTA	StL	L	E	66-13		Px	77	90	24	W, NP, LB, Blg
BATTLE	StL	L	E	63-14	L	Px	75			
BEAR	StL	L	E	63-14	L	Px	64			
BEAR TRAP	StL	K	E	65-12	L	Px	141	28	38	W, NP
BEARTRACK	StL	L	1	67-15	L	Px	169	25	55	Rb, Sf
BEAVER	L	T	E	63-6	L	Px	254	40	70	W, NP, Blg
BECOOSIN	L	K	E	63-8		Px	52			
BENCH	C	G	GM	64-2	L	P	28	93	10	Bt
BENEZIE	L	K	E	63-8		Px	59			
BESHO	L	T	F	60-6	L.		29	100	5	NP
BETH	c	T	F	62-5	L	Px	186	59	22	NP
BIBON	StL	L	E	66-13		Px				
BIG MOOSE	StL	L	E	64-14		Px	1,116	98	22	NP, SB
BIG RICE	StL	K	E	64-13	L	Px	416	100	6	NP, W, SB, Blg
BINGSCHICK	C	G	GM	65-4		Px	52		40	
BIRCH	L	K	E	64-8	L	Px	720	48	35	W, T, NP, SB
BOG	L	I	F	61-8		Px	317	96	16	NP, W
BOLOGNA	C	T	GM	64-4		Px	70			
BONNIE	L	K	E	65-7	L	Px	112	100	11	NP, Sf
BOOT	StL	K	E	65-12		Px	308	52	27	W, NP
BOOT	L	K	E	64-8	L	Px	216	64	83	W, NP, SB
BOOTLEG	StL	L	E	64-15		Px	352	37	26	SB

145

Lake Name	County	USFS Dist.	DNR Off.	Loc.	FP	Ace.	Acres	L	D	Fish
BOULDER	StL	L	E	63-14	L	Px	68	40	51	NP
BOULDER	L	T	E	64-6	L	Px	314	46	54	NP
BOW	L	T	E	63-7	L	P	98	100	7	NP, Blg
BOWER TROUT	C	G	GM	63-1	L	Px	136	100	6	W, NP, Sf
BOZE	L	T	F	63-6		Px	78			W, NP
BRANT	C	G	GM	65-4	L	Px	121	63	80	NP, Pch
BRIDGE	L	K	E	63-9		Px				W, NP
BRIGAND	StL	L	1	67-15		Px	23			
BRUIN	L	K	E	62-10	L	P	37		30	NP
BRULE	C	G	GM	63-2	M	Bi, Px	5,204	31	72	W, NP, SB
BUCK	StL	L	E	63-14	L	Px	228		19	W,NP
BULL	C	T	GM	63-2	L	P	67	79	33	NP
BULLET	L	K	E	65-11	L	P	47	100	10	W, NP, Blg
BULLFROG	L	K	E	65-6	L	Px	78	70	26	NP
BURNT	C	T	GM	62-4	L	Px	396	68	23	W,NP
CABIN	L	I	F	59-7	L		71	100	4	NP
CACABIC	L	K	E	63-7	L	P	22		30	NP
CACHE	L	K	E	63-8	L	P	40	100	15	NP
CALF	C	T	GM	63-2	L	No	19	96	18	Pch
CALICO	L	K	E	65-6	L	P	14	69	20	Sf
CAM	C	T	GM	63-3	L	P	66	49	57	N P, Pch
CAMDRE	L	K	E	62-9	L	P	51	100	12	None

Lake Name	County	USFS Dist.	DNR Off.	Loc.	FP	Acc.	Acres	L	D	Fish
CAMP	L	K	E	64-11	M	P	84		31	NP
CANOE	C	G	GM	64-1	L	P x	107		39	W, NP, SB
CANOE	L	K	E	65-6	L	P	22	70	30	Sf
CANTA	L	G	E	65-6	L	P	17		55	NP
CAP	L	T	E	64-6		P x	46			
CAREY(COXEY)	StL	K	E	64-13	L	P x	208	100	14	NP, SB, LB, Blg
CARL	C	G	GM	64-1		P x	45		20	Rt
CARIBOU	C	G	GM	65-1	L	P x	497	6	5	NP, LB, W
CAROL	L	K	E	63-7	L	P x	96	100	15	NP, W, Blg
CAT	L	I	F	60-9	L.	6	0	82	24	NP, W, LB, Ct, Blg
CATTYMAN	L	K	E	64-8	L	P	30	100	9	W, NP
CEDAR	L	K	E	63-11			472	34	45	W, NP, Sf
CHAD	StL	L	E	63-15	L	P x	277	100	18	NP, LB, Big
CHEROKEE	C	T	GM	63-4	L	P x	1,016	12	142	T, NP
CHERRY	L	K	E	65-6		P x	178	23	90	T, W
CHIPPEWA	L	K	E	66-11		P x	95			
CLAM	C	T	GM	63-4	L		67	96	19	NP
CLAM	L	K	E	65-6	L	P x	28	100	10	Sf
CLARK	StL	L	E	63-14	L	P x	72	37	44	LB, NP, Blg
CLEAR	L	K	E	63-10	M	P x	239	99	19	W, NP, Sf
CLEARWATER	C	G	GM	65-1	M	Bi, Px	1,537	20	130	T, SB

Lake Name	County	USFS Dist.	DNR Off.	Loc.	FP	Acc.	Acres	L	D	Fish
CLEARWATER	L	K	E	62-9	L	Px	615	27	46	NP
CLOVE	C	G	GM	65-4	L	Px	172		25	W, NP, SB
CONCHU	L	K	E	63-10		P	50	47	66	Bt
CONTENTMENT	StL	L	E	67-15	L	Px	44		50	NP
COOK COUNTY	L	K	E	65-5		P	49	62	38	Sf
COW	C	T	GM	63-2	L	P	46	49	36	Pch
CRAB	StL	L	E	63-13	L	Px	424	45	60	W, NP, SB, LB, Sf
CROCODILE	C	G	GM	64-1	L	Px	335	100	15	W, LB, Pch
CROOKED	C	G	GM	64-5	L	Px	321	47	75	T
CROOKED	StL	K	E	66-11		Px	10.904		165	W, SB, NP, LB, Ct, Sf
CROW	C	G	GM	63-2	L		52	100	6	NP
CRYSTAL	C	G	GM	64-1, 2	L	Px	210		80	W, T, Pch
CUMMINGS	StL	L	E	64-14	L	Px	1,139	41	46	NP, SB, Sf
CYPRESS (OTTERTRACK)	L	K	E	66-6	M	Px	1,092	22	116	T, NP, W, SB
DANIELS	C	G	GM	65-1		Px	529		90	T, NP, SB
DARK	StL	L	E	66-13		Px	38			
DAVIS	C	T	GM	64-3		Px	384	15	64	NP
DAWKINS	C	G	GM	64-3,4	L	P	77	79	19	W, NP, Pch
DEER	C	G	GM	64-1	L	Px	83		30	W, NP, LB
DELTA	L	K	E	63-9		Px				
DENT	C	T	F	63-5		Px	112			
DEVILS ELBOW	C	G	GM	664	L	Px	85		50	W, SB, NP

Lake Name	County	USFS Dist.	DNR Off.	Loc.	FP	Acc.	Acres	L	D	Fish
DIANA	L	I	F	62-8	L	x	52	100	13	W, NP, SF
DISAPPOINTMENT	L	K	E	63-8	L	Px	950	65	51	W, NP, LB
DIX	L	K	E	65-7		Px	119	8	54	NP, Sf
DOVRE	StL	1	1	67-16	L	Px	117	95	17	NP, W
DRUMSTICK	L	K	E	63-8		Px	19			
DUCK	StL	K	E	64-13		P	126	100	5	none
DUGOUT	Stl	L	E	63-15	L	Px	31	100	15	W, NP, Pch
DUNCAN	C	G	GM	65-1	L	Px	630	31	130	T, W, NP, SB
DUNN	C	G	GM	65-1	L	P	108		65	T
DUTTON	L	K	E	65-6	L	P	33	100	80	Pch
EAGLE	C	G	GM	63-2	L	P	89	100	14	NP, Pch
EAST DAWKINS	C	G	GM	64-3	L	P	80	77	15	W, NP, Pch
EAST KERFOOT	C	G	GM	65-4	L	P	13		26	Sf
EAST PIKE	C	G	GM	65-3	L	Px	563	100	50	SB, Msk
EAST PIPE	C	G	GM	62-3	L	P	136	100	12	W, NP
ECHO	C	T	GM	63-2	L	Px	142	33	12	W, NP, SB
EDDY	L	K	E	65-6	L	Px	134	50	86	T, NP
EDITH	C	G	GM	65-4	L	P	10	100	44	NP, Pch
ELLA	C	G	GM	62-5	L	Px	60	35	6	NP
ELLA HALL	L	K	E	64-10	M	Px	372		28	NP, SB, LB, Sf
ELM	C	G	GM	64-5		Px	126			

Lake Name	County	USFS Dist.	DNR Off.	Loc.	FP	Acc.	Acres	L	D	Fish
ELTON	L	T	E	64-6	L	P x	140	68	53	NP
EMERALD	StL	L	1	67-16	L	P x	66	34	17	Sf
ENSIGN	L	K	E	64-8	L	P x	1,583	43	30	W, NP, SB
ESKWAGAMA	L	K	E	62-10	L	P x	79	100	12	NP
ESTER	L	K	E	65-6		P x	458	40	110	T, NP
EUGENE	StL	L	1	67-15	L	P x	181	30	60	NP
EXPLORER	L	K	E	64-7	L	P x	59	26	75	T
FAITH	L	K	E	65-6	L		32	100	15	NP
FAIRY	StL	K	E	65-12	L	P x	101	74	19	W, NP, Sf
FALLEN ARCH	L	I	F	62-18	L		21	100	11	NP
FALL	L	K	E	63-11	H	Bi, P x	2,232	54	32	W, NP, Sf
FAN	C	G	GM	65-2		P	7	100	3	None
FAT	StL	L	1	67-15	L	P x	108	25	50	T
FAT (Mantle)	StL	L	E	67-14			29			NP
FAULT	C	G	GM	64-3	L	P	61	100	10	Sf
FAY	C	G	GM	65-5	L	P x	77	65	T	
FEE	L	T	E	64-6		P x	36			
FERN	C	G	GM	64-5	L	P x	79	30	70	T, NP
FERNE	L	I	F	62-7	L	P x	153	100	8	W, NP
FINGER	StL	L	E	67-14	L	P x	295	35	60	W
FIRE	L	K	E	63-8	L	P x	110	70	30	NP, Blg

Lake Name	County	USFS Dist.	DNR Off.	Loc.	FP	Acc.	Acres	L	D	Fish
FISH	L	K	E	65-6	L	P x	112	79	30	NP
FISHDANCE	L	K	E	63-7	L	P x	169	51	50	W, NP, Blg
FISHER (Oliver)	L	T	E	63-7	L	P x	79	47	25	LB, Blg
FLAME	C	T	GM	62-4	L	P x	56	75	22	N P, Pch
FOUND	L	K	E	64-9	M	P x	60	41	40	Rt, Spl
FOUR	L	K	E	63-8	L	P x	749	78	25	W, NP
FOURTOWN	L	K	E	64-11	L	P x	1,305	57	25	W, NP, SB
FOX	StL	L	E	66-13		P x	27	100	7	
FRASER	L	K	E	64-7	L	P x	811		80	T, NP, W
FREDERICK	C	T	G	63-5	L	P x	57	100	10	NP
FRENCH	C	G	GM	64-5	L	P x	128	15	135	T
FROG	L	K	E	64-8		P x	58	52	38	
FROST	C	T	GM	64-4	L	P x	313		80	T, NP, Pch
GABBRO	L	K	E	62-10	L	P x	1,174	51	50	W, NP, Cr, SB
GABIMICHIGAMI	C	G	GM	64-5	L	P x	1,236	12	209	T, NP, Pch
GADWALL	K	G	GM	64-2	L	P	21	38	52	Bt
GASKIN	C	G	GM	64-2	L	P x	451		65	T, W
GE-BE-ON-EQUAT	StL	L	E	67-14	L	P x	652	40	55	W, NP, Sf
GERALDINE	StL	K	E	63-13			44			NP
GERUND	L	K	E	64-7	L	P x	99	28	85	NP
GIBSON	L	K	E	64-8	L	P	36	71	24	W, NP

Lake Name	County	USFS Dist.	DNR Off.	Loc.	FP	Acc.	Acres	L	D	Fish
GIFT	L	K	E	65-6	L	Px	47	75	35	NP
GIJIKIKI	L	K	E	65-6		Px	124	22	82	T
GILLIS	C	G	GM	64-5	L	Px	703	13	180	T, NP
GLENMORE	StL	L	E	63-14	L	Px	56	100	8	NP, Big
GLIMMER	StL	L	E	63-14		Px	17	100	6	
GNEISS	C	G	GM	66-4	L	Px	220		70	T, W, NP, SB
GOGEBIC	C	G	GM	65-2	L	Px	61		61	Bt
GOOD	L	K	E	64-10	L	Px	183	35	51	NP, SB, W, Cr
GORDON	C	T	GM	64-4	L	Px	167		93	T, NP
GOWAN	StL	L	E	64-15		Px	158			NP
GRACE	C	T	F	62-5	L	Px	479	76	16	W, NP
GRANDPA	C	G	GM	66-5	L	P	133	48	55	NP, Pch
GRANITE	C	G	GM	65-4	L	Px	302		45	W, NP, SB
GREEN	StL	L	E	67-14	L	Px	153	53	20	NP, Blg
GREEN	C	T	GM	654	L	P	45	17	75	
GRUB	L	K	E	64-8	L	Px	41	56	31	SB, LB, Sf
GULF	C	G	GM	66-4	L	P	35	93	17	NP
GULL	StL	K	E	65-12	L	Px	196	100	13	NP, Sf
GULL	L	K	E	62-9	L	Px	495	72	31	W, NP, SB
GUMP	C	G	GM	66-5		P	13	100	11	none
GUN	StL	K	E	65-12	L	Px	358	30	57	W, NP, SB, Blg

Lake Name	County	USFS Dist.	DNR Off.	Loc.	FP	Acc.	Acres	L	D	Fish
GUN	StL	L	1	67-15	L	P x	202	15	135	T
HANDLE	c=C	T	GM	63-4	L	CW	15	100	7	N P, Pch
HANSON	L	K	E	65-6	L	P x	300	15	100	T, NP
HASSEL	StL	L	E	63-14	L	P x	76	100	5	NP, Blg
HATCHET	L	K	E	64-7	L	P x	158	85	40	W,NP
HAZEL	C	T	F	62-6		P x	125	100		NP
HEGMAN	StL	K	E	64-12	M	P	198	50	55	W,SB,NP
HENSON	C	G	GM	64-2		P x	146		30	NP
HERITAGE	StL	L	1	66-15	L	P x	205	50	40	W, NP, Rb, Pch
HILLY	C	T	GM	62-3	L	P	32	87	23	NP
HOE	L	T	E	64-6		P x	58			
HOLT	L	G	E	65-6	L	P	129	31	73	T, NP
HOME	StL	K	E	65-12	L	P x	85		24	W,NP
HOMER	C	T	GM	63-3	L	Bl, P x	516	90	22	W, NP, Pch
HOOK	StL	K	E	64-13	L	P x	92	100	13	NP
HOPE	L	I	E	62-7	L	P x	154	100	8	W,NP
HORSE	L	K	E	64-11	L	P x	724	55	25	W, NP, Blg
HORSEFISH	L	K	E	64-6		P x	51			NP
HORSESHOE	C	G	GM	64-1		P x	208		20	NP, W
HORSESHOE	L	K	E	62-9	L	P x	194	67	40	W, NP, Blg
HOWARD	C	G	GM	65-5	L	P x	170	24	175	T, Pch
HUB	C	T	GM	64-5		P x	123		20	NP

Lake Name	County	USFS Dist.	DNR Off.	Loc.	FP	Ace.	Acres	L	D	Fish
HUDSON	L	K	E	63-8	L	P x	374	59	35	W, NP, Big, W
HULA	L	K	E	64-10	L	P	121	100	4	NP
HUSTLER	StL	L	E	66-14	L	P x	294	45	74	NP, Blg
IMA	L	K	E	64-7	L	P x	863	27	116	W, NP
INDIANA	L	K	E	64-10	L	P x	153		31	NP, SB
INSULA	L	K	E	63-7	L	P x	2,550	40	63	W,NP
IRON	StL	L	E	66-12	L	P x	2,298		60	W, NP, SB
ISABELLA	L	I	F	61-7	L	P x	1,318	99	18	W, NP
JACK	C	T	GM	63-4	L	P x	127	100	10	W, NP, Pch
JACKFISH	L	K	E	65-11	L	P x	225	99	18	NP
JAP	C	G	GM	65-5	L	P x	146	33	60	Rt, T
JASPER	C	G	GM	65-5	L	P x	264	36	125	T, W. NP, SB
JENNY	L	K	E	65-6	L	P x	115	52	93	NP
JERRY	C	G	m	64-5	L	P x	91		47	NP
JIG	StL	L	E	63-13		P x	34			
JIMMY	C	G	GM	65-5	L	P	34		26	T
JITTERBUG	L	K	E	64-8	L	P	32	100	5	NP
JOHN	C	G	GM	64-3	L	P x	101	90	20	W,SB,NP
JONATHAN (Serenade)	StL	L	E	64-14			133			NP
JORDAN	L	K	E	64-8	L	P x	16	44	66	W,NP

Lake Name	County	USFS Dist.	DNR Off.	Loc.	FP	Acc.	Acres	L	D	Fish
JUG	L	T	E	64-6	L	P	43	100	6	NP
JUNO	C	T	GM	63-3	L	P x	243	94	23	NP, Pch, W
KARL	C	G	GM	64-3	L	P x	145		75	NP, T
KAWASACHONG	L	T	F	62-6	L	P x	177	100	11	W, NP
KAWISHIWI	L	T	F	62-6	L	Bl, P x	468	100	12	W, NP
KEKAKABIC	L	K	E	64-6	L	P x	1,905	61	195	T
KEKAKABIC POND	L	K	E	65-6	L	P	72	41	25	NP, T
KELLY	C	T	GM	62-4	L	P x	188	100	13	W, NP, Pch
KELSEY	StL	L	E	67-13		P x	30	62	22	
KELSO	C	T	F	63-5	L	P x	153	98	16	NP
KENEU	StL	L	E	64-13		P x	37		27	NP
KETTLE	L	K	E	65-7	L	P x	47	42	15	Sf
KIANA	L	K	E	63-7	L	P x	207	38	56	NP
KINOGAMI	C	T	GM	62-3	L		124	72	30	W, NP, LB, Pch
KIOWA	C	G	GM	64-2	L	no	32		29	NP
KISKADINA	C	G	GM	64-3		P x	139		40	NP
KIVANIVA	L	T	E	64-6	L	P x	34	80	49	W, NP
KNIFE	L	K	E	65-7	M	P x	5,536	20	130	W, T, NP, SB
KNIGHT	C	T	F	62-5, 6	L	P x	119	100	6	NP, Pch
KNUTE	StL	L	E	67-16		P x	14			
KOMA	L	T	F	65-6	L	P x	266	100	14	W, NP, Blg
KORB	StL	L	E	63-14	L	P x	62	51	27	SB, NP, LB, Blg

Lake Name	County	USFS Dist.	DNR Off.	Loc.	FP	Acc.	Acres	L	D	Fish
KROFT	C	G	GM	63-1	L	P	25	100	11	
LA POND	StL	K	E	64-13	L	P x	176	100	4	NP
LAC	C	G	GM	63-1	L	P	72	80	20	NP
LAC LA CROIX	StL	L	E	66-13		P x	34,070		180	T,W,NP,SB,Stg,Cr,Rb
LAKE OF THE CLOUDS	L	K	E	65-6	L	P	32	51	110	T
LAMB	StL	L	E	66-14		P	139		18	NP
LARCH	C	G	GM	65-4	L	P x	142	100	14	N P, Pch
LEDGE	L	T	E	64-6	L	P x	23			
LILY	C	T	G M	63-3	L	P	22	62	53	N P
LINK	L	K	E	65-6	L	P	45	42	30	N P
LITTLE BEARTRACK	StL	L	1	67-15	L	P x	48	30	35	Rb, Sf
LITTLE CARIBOU	C	G	GM	65-1	L	P x	56	85	18	LB, NP, Pch
LITTLE CRAB	StL	L	E	63-14	L	P x	62	100	15	Blg
LITTLE GABBRO	L	K	E	62-10	L	P x	228	76	26	W, NP, Cr
LITTLE HUSTLER (Ruby)	StL	L	E	66-14		P x	72	43	70	NP, Sf
LITTLE KEKEKABIC	L	K	E	65-6	L	P x	62	9	142	T
LITTLE KNIFE	L	K	E	65-6		P x	680	14	184	W,T,NP,SB
LITTLE LOON	StL	L	1	67-15	L	P x	175	15	65	W, NP, SB, Sf, Rb
LITTLE MAYHEW	C	G	GM	65-2	L	P	41	57	31	Rt
LITTLE NORTH	C	G	GM	65-2	L	P	104	86	23	W, NP, T, SB

Lake Name	County	USFS Dist.	DNR Off.	Loc.	FP	Acc.	Acres	L	D	Fish
LITTLE RICE	StL	K	E	64-13		P	161	100	5	NP
LITTLE RUSH	C	G	GM	64-2	L	P	19	100	7	W, NP, Pch
LITTLE SAGANAGA	C	G	GM	64-5	L	P x	1,962		150	T, NP
LITTLE SHELL	StL	L	E	66-15	L	P x	90	48	40	W, Blg, Rb
LITTLE TROUT	C	G	GM	63-1	L	P x	147	57	56	T
LITTLE TROUT	StL	L	E	64-15	L	P x	665	33	37	W, NP, SB
LITTLE VERMILION	StL	L	1	67-16	M	BI P x	1,331	48	52	W, NP, SB, Pch, Stg
LIZZ	C	G	GM	64-1	L	P	25	71	30	W, NP
LONG	C	G	GM	64-3	L	P	140	70	24	NP
LONG ISLAND	C	G	GM	64-3	L	P x	971		69	T, NP
LOON	StL	L	1	66-15	L	P x	3,101	35	75	W, NP, SB, Sf, Rb
LOUIS	StL	K	E	64-12	M	P	30	45	52	Rt, Bt
LOWER PAUNESS	StL	L	E	66-15	L	P x	215	75	35	W, NP, SB, Rb
LUM	C	G	GM	64-2	L	P	36	87	18	T
LUNAR	L	K	E	65-6	L	P	72	43	60	T
LUNETTA	StL	L	E	63-14	L	P x	102	100	14	NP, SB, LB, Sf
LUX	C	G	GM	64-1		P x	51		20	Bt
LYNX	StL	L	E	66-14	L	P x	282	5	85	W,NP
MAKWA	L	T	E	64-6	L	P x	146	29	76	T, NP
MALBERG	L	T	E	63-6	L	P x	442	77	37	W,NP
MANIWAKI	L	K	F	62-7	L	P x	114	100	0	NP, Msk

Lake Name	County	USFS Dist.	DNR Off.	Loc.	FP	Acc.	Acres	L	D	Fish
MANOMIN	L	K	E	64-9	L	Px	455	99	18	NP
MARABOEUF	C	G	GM	66-4	L	Px	902		55	W, NP, SB
MARATHON	L	I	F	62-8	L	P	37	100	11	NP
MARSHALL	C	G	GM	63-1	L	Px	62	98	16	W, NP, SB
MAVIS	C	G	GM	64-4	L	P	10	32	55	Bt
MAXINE	StL	L	E	63-13		Px	38			
MEAT	StL	L	E	63-14	L	Px	28	96	24	NP
MEDAS	L	K	E	64-7		Px	22			
MEDITATION	C	G	GM	65-4	L	P	32	44	31	Rt, Bt
MEEDS	C	G	GM	64-2		Px	408		41	W
MERRITT	StL	L	E	63-16		Px	202	100	8	NP
MESABA	C	T	F	63-5	L	Px	258	15	65	NP, T
MIDAS	L	K	E	65-6	L	P	20		50	NP
MIDDLE CONE	C	T	GM	63-3	L	Px	81	51	30	W, NP, SB
MIDGET	C	T	GM	62-4	L	P	25	77	24	NP
MISPLACED	C	G	GM	64-2	L	P	81	96	18	
MISQUAH	C	G	GM	64-1	L	Px	57	27	60	T, Bt
MISSING LINK	C	G	GM	64-4	L	Px	41	62	25	Rt, Bt
MISSIONARY	L	K	E	64-7	L	Px	110	28	70	T
MOIYAKA	L	K	E	64-7		Px	49			NP
MOON	C	G	GM	64-1	L	P	156		30	NP, W, LB, Pch
MOOSE	C	G	GM	65-3	L	Px	1,030		118	T, W

158

Lake Name	County	USFS Dist.	DNR Off.	Loc.	FP	Acc.	Acres	L	D	Fish
MOOSE	L	K	E	64-9	H	Bl P x	1,307	99	65	W, NP, SB
MOOSECAMP	L	K	E	65-11	L	P x	187		16	W, NP, Blg
MORA	C	G	GM	64-5		P x	247		45	NP
MORGAN	C	G	GM	64-1	L	P	89			
MORRIS	C	G	GM	66-4	L	P	69		22	NP
MOUNTAIN	C	G	GM	65-2	M	P x	1,980	24	210	T
MUD	L	K	E	64-10	L	P x	164	88	17	NP
MUDRO	StL	K	E	64-12	L	P x	80	5	76	T, W, NP, SB
MUELLER	L	G	E	65-6	L	P x	30	97	36	W
MULE	StL	L	E	65-13		P	54	100	10	
MULLIGAN	C	T	GM	63-3	L	P x	31	40	62	Bt, Rt
MUSKEG	L	K	E	64-11	L	P	178	100	7	NP
MUSKEG	C	G	GM	64-3		P x	37		47	
MUSKRAT	L	K	E	64-7	L	P	15	75	18	W
MUZZLE	L	K	E	64-8		P x	72			
NABEK	L	G	E	65-6	L	P	48		65	none
NAHIMANA	StL	L	E	67-14		P x	45			
NAWAKWA	L	K	E	65-6	L	P x	103	100	9	NP
NEESH	StL	L	E	64-14			39	100	6	NP
NEEWIN	StL	L	E	64-14		P x	100	100	15	NP
NEGLIGE	L	K	E	65-6	L	P x	36		58	Bt
NEWFOUND	L	K	E	64-9	M	Bl P x	652	29	45	W, NP, SB

159

Lake Name	County	USFS Dist.	DNR Off.	Loc.	FP	Acc.	Acres	L	D	Fish
NEWTON	L	K	E	63-11	M	P x	502	72	47	W, NP, SB, Cr
NBIN	StL	L	E	66-13		P x	41		11	NP, W
NIGHTHAWK	C	G	GM	64-1		P	20	100		NP
NIKI	L	K	E	65-11		P x	56			NP
NINA MOOSE	StL	L	E	64-14	L	P x	430	100	6	W, NP, SB
NISWI	StL	L	E	64-14		P x	119	100	8	NP
NORTH	C	G	GM	65-2	L	P x	2,685	18	125	T, W, NP, SB
NORTH	StL	L	1	67-15	L	P x	163	100	10	W, NP, Cr, SB, Sf
NORTH CONE	C	T	GM	63-3	L	P x	90	29	53	W, NP, SB
NORTH FOWL	C	G	GM	65-3	M	P x	1,094	100	10	W, NP, SB
NORTH KERFOOT	C	G	GM	65-4		P	16	100	7	none
NORTH TEMPERANCE	C	T	GM	63-3	L	P x	258	47	53	NP
NORTH WILDER	L	K	F	62-8	L	P x	103	81	25	W, NP, Big
NORWAY	StL	L	1	67-15	L	P	58	40	37	N P, Pch
OGISHKEMUNCIE	L	G	E	65-6	L	P x	893	42	70	T, W, NP, SB
OMEGA (OGEMA)	C	G	GM	64-2		P x	196		51	NP
ONE	L	K	E	63-9	L	P x	822	52	57	W,NP
ONE ISLAND	C	G	GM	64-2	L	P	28	95	25	NP, Pch
ORINIAK	StL	L	E	64-16		P x	748	82	17	W,NP
OTTER	StL	L	E	64-14		P x	78	98	17	NP, SB, Sf
OWL	C	G	GM	64-5	L	P	80	37	70	T

Lake Name	County	USFS Dist.	DNR Off.	Loc.	FP	Acc.	Acres	L	D	Fish
OYSTER	StL	L	E	66-14	L	P x	772	32	130	T, NP, SB
PADDLE	C	G	GM	64-1	L	CW	21	100	16	NP, W, SB
PAGAMI	L	K	E	62-9	L	CW	75	100	7	W, NP
PAGEANT	StL	L	1	67-15	L	P x	60			
PAKWENE	L	K	E	65-11		P x	25			NP
PAN	L	T	E	64-6	L	P x	106	47	58	W,NP
PANHANDLE	L	T	E	64-6	L	P	14	85	22	NP
PAPOOSE	L	K	E	66-11			54			SB,LB
PARENT	L	K	E	63-8	L	P x	412	28	50	W,NP
PARTRIDGE	C	G	GM	65-1	L	P x	133	19	80	T
PEKAN	StL	L	E	67-14	L	P x	36		23	NP, Sf
PEMMICAN	C	G	GM	65-2	L	P	27	18	51	Bt
PERENT	L	I	F	61-6	L	P x	1,844	76	38	W,NP
PETER	C	G	GM	64-5	L	P x	294	27	120	T
PETERSON	C	T	GM	62-4	L	P x	104	98	15	W, NP, Pch
PHANTOM	StL	L	E	63-14	L	P x	52	100	10	NP
PHOEBE	C	T	F	62-5, 6	L	P x	758	62	25	W,NP
PICKLE	L	K	E	65-7	L	P x	104	34	22	NP
PIE	C	T	F	63-5	L	P	63	100	10	NP
PIERZ	C	G	GM	64-2	L	P x	93	58	28	none
PIETRO	L	K	E	62-9	L	P x	325	21	31	NP, W
PILLSBERRY	C	G	GM	64-2		P x	76	20		

Lake Name	County	USFS Dist.	DNR Off.	Loc.	FP	Acc.	Acres	L	D	Fish
PINE	StL	L	E	63-15	L	Px	912	16	18	W, NP, Sf
PINE	C	G	GM	64-3		Px	2,112	52	113	T, W, SB
PIPE	C	T	GM	62-3		Px	18		33	NP, Pch
POCKET	StL	L	E	67-14	L	Px	258	38	25	W, NP
POLLY	L	T	F	63-6	L	Px	541	80	21	W, NP, Sf
PORTAGE	L	K	E	65-8	L	P	67		45	SB,NP
POSE	L	K	F	62-8		Px	87		12	NP
POSSE	StL	L	E	67-14		Px	15	100		
POWELL	C	G	GM	64-5	L	P	58	41	75	T
POW-WOW	L	I	F	62-7	L	P	22	72	42	NP
PRAYER	C	G	GM	66-4	L	P	43		19	NP
PROFIT	StL	L	E	67-14	L	P	15	100	12	NP
PUP	C	G	GM	64-3		P	44	60	43	NP
QUADGA	L	I	F	62-9	L	Px	236	64	30	W, NP, Sf
RABBIT	L	K	E	66-6		Px	130	19	105	T
RAILROAD	L	I	F	58-10			11	100	4	none
RAM	C	G	GM	63-1	L	Px	73	42	40	T, Rt
RAMSHEAD	StL	L	E	66-14	L	Px	542	100	10	W,NP
RANGE	L	K	E	64-11	L	Px	100	67	19	W, NP, LB, Sf
RANGE LINE	StL	L	E	67-14	L	Px	123	58	57	T
RAT	C	G	GM	65-1		Px	34	100	5	
RATTLE	C	G	GM	64-5		P	50	62	30	SB

Lake Name	County	USFS Dist.	DNR Off.	Loc.	FP	Acc.	Acres	L	D	Fish
RAVEN	L	T	E	64-6	L	P x	204	34	56	T
RED ROCK	C	G	GM	65-5	L	P x	464	41	64	W, NP, SB
REDFIN	L	K	E	64-7	L	P	15	100	15	LB
REWARD	C	G	GM	66-4	L	no	21	100	14	NP
RIB	C	G	GM	64-4		P x	94	100	10	NP
RICE	L	I	F	62-8		P x	206	100	3	W, NP
RICE	StL	K	E	64-13		P x			18	
RIFLE	L	K	E	63-9	L	P x	36	69	18	NP
RITUAL	StL	K	E	66-12	L		64	36	40	NP
ROCK ISLAND	L	K	E	63-9	L	P x	65	64	21	NP
ROCKY	C	G	GM	64-1	L	P	83	27	35	NP
ROCKY	StL	L	E	66-14	L	P x	122	36	40	SB, NP
ROE	L	T	E	64-6	L	P	76	100	7	NP
ROG	C	G	GM	65-5	L	P x	55	41	40	Bt
ROMANCE	C	G	GM	66-4	L	P	168	60	32	NP
ROSE	C	G	GM	65-1	L	P x	1,404	31	90	T, W, SB
ROVE	C	G	GM	65-1	L	P	74	70	30	SB
ROY	C	G	GM	66-5	L	P	66	60	45	NP
ROYAL	C	G	GM	64-3		P	25			W
RUBY	StL	L	E	66-14		P x	316		70	NP, Sf, T
RUSH	C	G	GM	64-2	L	P x		50	54	NP
RUSH	StL	L	E	66-13		P x	119	100	10	NP, W, SB, Rb
SACA	StL	L	E	63-14	L	P x	98	93	18	NP, SB, Sf
SAGANAGA	C	G	GM	66-4	M	BI, P x	19,610		280	T, W, NP, SB

Lake Name	County	USFS Dist.	DNR Off.	Loc.	FP	Acc.	Acres	L	D	Fish
SAGUS	L	K	E	64-6	L	P x	188	60	37	NP, W
SANDPIT	L	K	E	64-11	L	P x	65	29	53	W, NP, Blg
SAWBILL	C	T	GM	62-4	M	Bl, P xx	944	58	44	W, NP, SB, Rb
SCHLAMM	StL	L	E	63-14	L	P x	69	100	6	NP, Big
SECOND 3 POND	StL	L	I	67-15		P x				
SEAGULL	C	G	GM	65-4	M	Bl, P xx	4.996	23	145	T, W, NP, SB
SEDATIVE	L	K	E	64-7	L	P x	85	80	27	NP
SEED	L	K	E	65-8	L	P	89	100	10	SB, W
SEMA	L	K	E	65-7	L	P x	78	17	72	T
SHADOW	C	G	GM	66-4	L		14	70	23	Sf
SHALLOW	L	K	E	64-8	L	P	16	100	5	
SHELL	StL	L	E	66-15	L	P x	525	100	15	W, NP, Sf, Rb
SHEPO	L	K	E	64-7	L	P x	58	82	17	W,NP
SHRIKE	C	G	GM	62-2	L		32	100	12	NP
SILICA	StL	L	E	64-13	L	P x	47	96	16	NP, SB, Sf
SINNEEG	StL	K	E	65-12	L					W
SKIDWAY	C	G	GM	63-1	L	P, CW	20	100	14	W, NP, Pch
SKINDANCE	L	G	E	65-6	L	P x	58	52	52	NP
SKIPPER	C	G	GM	64-2	L	P x	126	37	30	W, NP, Pch
SKOOP	C	T	GM	63-4	L	P	11		17	NP
SKOOTA	L	K	E	64-7	L	P x	147	10	68	Pch
SKULL	L	K	E	64-9	M	P	29	57	38	Bt
SLIM	StL	K	E	64-13	M	P x	368	29	49	W, NP, Sf

Lake Name	County	USFS Dist.	DNR Off.	Loc.	FP	Ace.	Acres	L	D	Fish
SLIM	StL	L	1	67-15	L	Px	140	60	42	NP
SMITE	L	T	E	64-7	L	P	47	82	22	W, NP, Sf
SMOKE	C	T	GM	62-4	L	Px	186	82	20	NP, W, SB
SNIPE	C	G	GM	64-4	L	Px	135		80	
SNOWBANK	L	K	E	63-8	M	BI, Px	4,819	26	145	T, W, NP, SB
SOCK	C	G	GM	65-2	L	Px	27	80	23	Rt, Bt
SOLITUDE	L	K	E	64-8		Px	65			
SOUTH	C	G	GM	65-1	L	Px	1,143	14	140	T, NP, SB
SOUTH	StL	L	1	67-15	L	Px	40	100	10	NP
SOUTH CONE	C	T	GM	63-3	L	Px	79	86	21	W, NP, SB
SOUTH FARM	L	K	E	62-11	M	BI, Px	618	58	30	W, NP, Sf
SOUTH HOPE	L	K	F	62-7		Px	88	100	9	W, NP
SO. TEMPERANCE	C	T	GM	63-3	L	Px	258	74	24	W, NP
SOUTH WILDER	L	K	F	62-8	L	Px	75	48	36	W, NP
SPAULDING	C	G	GM	64-2	L	P	47	68	36	none
SPICE	L	G	E	65-6	L	Px	26	69	27	NP
SPIDER	L	K	E	64-7	L	Px	33	10	65	NP
SPLASH	L	K	E	64-8	L	Px	103	83	18	W, NP, Big
SPOON	L	K	E	65-7	L	Px	285	39	85	NP
SQUARE	L	T	F	62-6	L	Px	125	100	7	W, NP
SQUIRE	C	T	GM	63-3	L	P	89	100	7	NP
STEEP	StL	L	1	67-15	L	Px	98	40	40	NP, Sf

Lake Name	County	USFS Dist.	DNR Off.	Loc.	FP	Acc.	Acres	L	D	Fish
STEM	C	T	GM	62-3	L	no	45	85	34	NP
STERLING	StL	L	E	66-13		Px	180			
STRUP	L	K	E	64-7	L	Px	79	26	105	T, LB
STUART	StL	L	E	66-13	L	Px	804	31	40	NP, SB, Sf, W, LB
SUCKER	L	K	E	64-8	L	Px	353	47	30	W, NP, LB, SB
SUNDAY	StL	K	E	66-12			124			NP
SUNHIGH	C	C	F	62-5		Px	54	100	14	NP
SUNLOW	C	C	F	62-5		no	31	100	6	NP
SWAMP	C	C	GM	64-1	L	P	208	100	19	NP. W, Pch
SWAN	C	C	GM	63-2	L.	Px	219	27	108	W, NP
SWING	L	K	E	64-8	L	P	13	100	13	NP
TABLE	C	G	GM	64-2	L	P	11	100	5	none
TAKUCMICH	StL	L	E	67-14	L	Px	367	30	150	T, NP, SB, LB, Sf
TENOR	C	G	GM	66-4	L	P	21	100	11	NP, W, SB
TEPEE	C	G	GM	66-4	L	P	96	85	22	NP, Pch
TESOKER	StL	L	E	68-14	L	Px	22	25	37	LB, Sf
THIRTY-THREE	L	K	E	64-11	L	P	31	100	9	NP
THOMAS	L	K	E	63-7	M	Px	1,721	30	110	T, W, NP
THREE	L	K	E	62-9		Px	1,085	44	37	NP, W, Sf
THREE EAGLE	L	K	E	64-8		Px	60			
THUMB	StL	L	E	66-14			10	100	6	none
THUMB	StL	L	E	67-14	L	Px	72	58	55	NP, W
THUNDER	StL	K	E	65-12	L	Px	169	66	52	W, NP
TICKLE	L	G	E	65-5	L	P	49	48	61	NP

166

Lake Name	County	USFS Dist.	DNR Off.	Loc.	FP	Acc.	Acres	L	D	Fish
TIN CAN MIKE	L	K	E	64-11	L	P x	142	64	29	SP, Blg
TOBACCO	C	T	GM	62-3	L	P	18	100	9	NP
TOE	StL	L	E	67-13		P x	484	25	57	
TOE	L	K	E	65-6	L	P x	52	30	44	NP
TOMAHAWK	L	I	F	62-7		P	50	100	9	
TOPAZ	L	K	E	65-6	L	P x	174	22	70	T, W, SB
TOPPER	C	G	GM	65-2	L	P x	51	75	28	Bt
TORNADO	L	K	F	62-8			25	100	7	NP
TOTEM	L	K	E	66-6	L	P	18	100	19	NP
TOWN	C	T	GM	63-3	L	P x	94		60	NP
TRADER	L	K	E	64-8	L	P	89	100	10	NP
TRAIL	L	T	F	63-6		P x	62			W, NP
TRAP	C	G	GM	64-1			71	100	9	none
TRAPLINE	L	T	E			P x	23			
TREASE	StL	K	E	64-12			26		53	NP
TREASURE	L	T	E	64-6	L	P	32	43	20	NP
TREMOLO	L	K	E	62-8	L	P	31	64	14	NP
TRIDENT	L	K	E	64-8		P x	99	100	38	
TRILLIUM	StL	L	E	67-14	L	P x	36	25	98	LB
TROUT	StL	L	E	63-16	H	P x	9,237	21	35	T, NP, W, SB
TRYGG	StL	L	E	68-14	L	P x	30	32	42	Bt
TUCKER	C	G	GM	64-3	L	P	168	55		W,NP

Lake Name	County	USFS Dist.	DNR Off.	Loc.	FP	Acc.	Acre.%	t,	D	Fish
TURTLE	L	K	E	62-10	L	P x	359	100	10	NP
TUSCARORA	C	T	GM	64-4	L	P x	866	24	130	T, NP
TWO	L	K	E	63-9		P x	529	33	35	W, NP
UNKNOWN	C	G	GM	63-3	L	P	9		36	Bt
UPPER HEGMAN	StL	K	E	64-12	M	P	100	59	30	W, SB, NP
UPPER PAUNESS	StL	L	E	66-15		P x	162	100	10	W, NP
VALE	C	G	GM	64-2	L	P	94	42	42	Bt
VASEUX	C	G	GM	65-2	L	P	11	100	10	none
VERA	L	K	E	64-8	L	P x	262	30	55	W, NP
VERN	C	T	GM	63-2	L	P x	230	34	42	W, NP
VERNON	C	T	GM	63-2	L	P x	295	30	101	W, NP, SB
VIREO	C	G	GM	63-2		P	12	100	13	
VIRGIN	C	G	GM	64-5	L	P x	60	39	40	none
VISTA	C	G	GM	64-1		P x	181	40	NP	
WAGER	L	I	F	62-8	L	P	14	100	11	NP, W
WAGOSH	StL	K	E	65-12		P x	49		8	W
WASHTE	L	K	E	64-9	L		84	100		none
WATAP	C	G	GM	65-1	L	P x	182		45	SB, NP
WATONWAN	L	T	F	62-6		P	64	80	25	W, NP
WEE	C	T	GM	62-4	L	P	13	77	34	Bt
WEIRD	C	T	GM	63-4	L	P x	47	100	6	W, NP

Lake Name	County	USFS Dist.	DNR Off.	Loc.	FP	Acc.	Acres	1,	D	Fish
WENCH	C	T	GM	63-3	L	P	25	47	59	Bt
WEST BEARSKIN	C	G	GM	65-1	M	Bi, P	522	20	78	NP, W, T, SB
WEST CRAB	StL	L	E	63-14			124			
WEST FERN	C	G	GM	64-5	L	P x	88	21	70	T
WEST KERFOOT	C	G	GM	65-4	L	P	26	100	15	LB, Sf
WEST OTTO	C	G	GM	64-2		P x	61		40	W
WEST PIKE	C	G	GM	65-2	L	P x	762	32	120	T, SB
WEST PIPE	C	G	GM	62-3	L	P	20	100	6	NP
WESTERN	StL	L	E	63-14	L	P x	135	100	12	W, NP
WHACK	C	T	GM	63-3	L	P	34	76	27	NP
WHALE	C	G	GM	63-2	L	P x	28	100	13	NP, Pch
WHIP	C	T	GM	63-3	L	P	38	100	9	NP, Pch
WHIPPED	C	T	GM	64-5		P x	62		5	NP
WHISKER	C	G	GM	63-2			30	100	6	none
WHITE FEATHER	StL	L	E	65-13		P x	108	100	6	NP
WHIZ	L	T	E	63-7	L	P	24		44	NP, Blg
WINCHELL	C	G	GM	64-2	L	P x	1,002	27	160	T, NP
WIND	L	K	E	64-9	L	P x	952	68	32	W, LB, NP, Sf
WINE	C	T	F	63-5	L	P x	294	50	65	T
WISINI	L	K	E	64-7	L	P x	129	8	137	T, LB
WITNESS	L	K	E	64-9	L	P	42	88	19	Pch

Lake Name	County	USFS Dist.	DNR Off.	Loc.	FP	Acc.	Acres	L	D	Fish
WONDER	C	T	F	62-5	L	82	100	10	NP	
WOOD	L	K	E	64-10	L	P	587	90	21	W, NP, SB, Blg
YODELER	StL	L	1	67-15	L	Px	44			
ZENITH	C	T	F	63-5		Px	24	78	20	Rb
ZEPHYR	C	G	GM	66-5	L	Px	155		40	W, NP, SB
ZOO	C	G	GM	62-2	L	P	104	89	26	NP

QUETICO PROVINCIAL PARK LAKE INDEX

Lake Name	Acres	Fish	Lake Name	Acres	Fish
AGNES	7397	T, NP, SB, W	BOCK	138	T
ALICE	1269	NP	BRENT	2159	T, NP, W, LB
ANCHOR	84	LB	BREWER	252	NP, SB, LB, W, Rb
ANTOINE	568	T, NP	BUCKINGHAM	627	T, NP, W
ANUBIS	153	NP, SB, W	BUD	276	NP, SB, W
ARGO	2364	T, NP	BURKE	650	T, NP, SB, LB, W, Rb
ART	247	NP, W	BURNTSIDE	1297	NP, SB, W, T
BADWATER	477	W, NP	BURT	1749	T, NP, LB, W
BALLARD	279	NP, SB, LB, W, SE	CACHE	1089	T, NP, SB
BAPTISM	563	NP, W	CAIRN	422	NP, SB, W
BART	393	NP, W, SB, LB Sf	CAMEL	477	NP, W
BASSWOOD	14730	T, NP, W, SB, LB, Sf, RB	CARP	1101	T, NP, WB, W
BATCHEWAUNG	2638	T, NP, SB, W	CEPH	42	NP, W, SB, Sf
BEARPELT	573	W, NP	CHATTERTON	692	NP, W, Rb
BEAVERHOUSE	4945	T, NP, W, SB, Rb	CIRRUS	5224	T, NP, SB, W, Cr, Sf
BEG	225	NP, W, SB	CLAIR	168	NP, W
BELL	153	Sf, Cr	CONE	160	T
BENTPINE	1015	NP, W, Rb	CONK	279	NP
BIRCH	711	T, NP, SB, W	CONMEE	1242	NP, W
BIRD	281	NP, W, SB	CROOKED	8647	NP, SB, LB, W, Sf, Cr
BISK	200	NP, SB, W	CUB	163	NP, W
BIT	104	NP, W	DAHLIN	173	SB, NP, Rb

171

Lake	Acres	Fish
DARKY	1230	T, NP, SB, W, Sf, Cr
DEER	–	W
DELAHEY	699	NP, W
DELL	62	NP, LB
DORE	731	T, NP
DRAPER	422	T, NP, W
EAST	212	NP, SB, W
EDGE	84	NP
ELIZABETH	326	NP, W
ELK	306	T
EMERALD	640	T
FERGUSON	1010	T, NP
FERN	325	NP, SB, W
FRED	793	NP, SB, W
FRENCH	746	T, NP, SB, W
GLACIER	306	T, SB, W
GOODIER	136	T
GRATTON	64	LB
GREY	79	SB, LB
HERONSHAW	257	W, NP
HOP	15	Bt
HOWARD	215	NP

Lake	Acres	Fish
IRON	2298	NP, SB, W
ISABELLA	128	NP, SB, LB, W
JACK	185	NP, W
JEAN	2176	T, NP, SB, W, Blg
JEFF	281	T, NP, SB
JESSE	800	NP, W
JOYCE	973	T, NP, W
KAHSHAHPIWI	1203	T, NP, SB, W
KASAKOKWOG	1902	T, NP, SB, W
KAWNIPI	9035	T, NP, W, SB
KEATS	358	NP, W
KEEFER	538	T, NP, SB, W
KEEWATIN	158	NP, SB, W
KENNEY	257	NP, W
KETT	257	T, NP
KNIFE	5536	T, NP, SB, W
LAC LA CROIX	34070	T, NP, SB, W, Stg, Cr, Rb
LAKIN	190	NP
LEMAY	385	W, NP
LILYPAD	62	NP, SB, W
LITTLE KNIFE	1680	T, NP, SB, W
LITTLE NEWT	59	LB

Lake	Acres	Fish
LITTLE PINE	136	NP
LITTLE ROLAND	54	SB, NP, Sf
LONELY	976	NP, SB, W
LOUISA	1773	T, NP
LYNX	86	NP
MACK	1882	NP, LB, W
MARIA	299	NP, W
MARJ	563	T
MEADOWS	183	SB, LB, Cr, Sf
MIDDLE ROLAND	158	NP, SB
MILT	170	LB, T
MINN	1146	NP, SB, W, Rb
MONTGOMERY	309	W, NP
MURDOCK	731	NP, W
MCALPINE	743	T, NP, W
MCAREE	2183	T, NP, SB, W, Rb, Sf
MCDOUGALL	943	T, NP
MCEWEN	1267	T, NP, SB, W
MCNAUGHT	133	NP, SB, LB, Blg
MCNIECE	153	T, NP
NEST	165	T, NP
NO MAN	62	T, NP, W

Lake	Acres	Fish
NOON	163	SB, LB
OLIPHAUNT	1367	T, NP, SB, W
OMEME	328	NP, W
ORIANA	963	NP, LB, W, T, Rb
OTHER MAN	442	T, W, NP, SB
OTTERTRACK (Cypress)	1092	T, NP, SB, W
PAULETTE	175	LB
PICKEREL	7314	T, NP, SB, W
PLOUGH	153	T, NP
POACHER	306	T, NP
POINT	101	NP, SB
POND	190	T, NP, Sb
POOHBAH	3366	T, NP, W, Rb
PULLING	79	SB, LB, Rb
QUETICO	10535	T, NP, SB, W, Sf
RAM	198	T, NP
RAWN	830	T, NP, SB, W
ROBIN	200	NP, W, Sf
ROBINSON	1030	T, NP, W, SB, LB
ROLAND	568	T, NP, W
ROUGE	163	NP, SB, W, Rb
RUSSELL	2445	NP, SB, W

Lake	Acres	Fish
SAGANAGA	19610	T, NP, SB, W
SAGANAGONS	5350	T, NP, SB, W
SARAH	2848	T, NP, SB, W, LB
SARK	701	T, NP, SB, W
SHADE	435	T, NP, W, SB, LB, Rb
SHELLY	741	NP, W
SHERIDAN	230	T, NP
SIDE	52	T, NP
SILENCE	570	T, NP, SB, W, LB, Rb
SLATE	180	NP, SB, W, Rb
SMALLY	–	LB, Sf
SMUDGE	111	NP, W
SOHO	670	T, NP, W
STURGEON	10058	T, NP, SB, W, Rb, Stg
SUCKER	–	NP, W
SULTRY	153	NP, W
SUMMER	153	T, NP, W
SUNDAY	1037	T, NP, SB, W, LB, CR, SF
SUZANETTE	691	W
TANNER	985	NP, SB, W
TED	309	T, NP, W
THAT MAN	385	T, SB, W, NP, Cr
THIS MAN	776	T, NP, W, Cr, Sf
TRANT	198	LB
TROUSERS	504	NP
TUCK	691	T, NP, W
VERON	655	NP, W
WALTER	776	T, NP, SB, W, Rb
WEST	101	NP, LB, W
WET	741	NP, W
WICKSTEED	1489	NP, SB, Sf, Rb
WILDGOOSE	240	NP, W
WILLIAM	444	W, NP
WOLSELEY	3278	T, NP, SB, W
WOODSIDE	286	W
YEH	89	NP, LB, W, Sf
YOUR	487	NP, W, Sf, Rb
YUM YUM	128	T, NP, SB, W

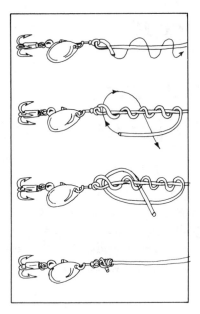

Improved Clinch Knot

The improved clinch knot is the best for tying line directly to lures, swivels. Wet line will slide easier, make stronger knot.

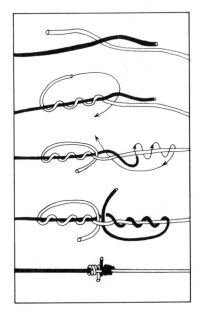

Blood Knot

The blood knot is used for joining lines of equal, or nearly equal, diameters. It is very strong and useful for adding line to your spool or tying on leaders. After knot is completely tight, clip off ends to avoid hangups in rod guides, spool or weeds.

Chapter 10

No Maid Service
in the Wilderness

THE CROOKED LAKE U.S. FOREST SERVICE cabin
sits at the bottom of Lower Basswood Falls. Two campsites are
within a few hundred yards of the cabin and as was my habit
the summer my wife Mary Jo and I spent based at the cabin as
volunteer Wilderness Rangers, I took our "ranger dog" Gypsy
on a walk to the sites, making my rounds.

The site behind the cabin, just above the roaring cataract
is a beautiful location, deep in needles beneath magnificent
pines. As I topped the hogback ridge behind the campsite I
spotted some newly arrived campers relaxing after the task of
making a snug camp. I also noticed that a large patch of caribou
moss that formerly resided on the rocky ridge was missing.

The campers were all middle-aged adults from a church
group and very friendly. After making our introductions and
examining their BWCAW permit I casually asked if anyone in
the group knew where that caribou moss had disappeared to.
Silence fell.

I guess they were a bit surprised, wondering how in the
world this guy knew that in this entire wilderness some moss
was missing.   Two men toed the ground sheepishly, avoiding
eye contact.

"Don't suppose that moss would be under one of your
tents, would it?" I asked, breaking the awkward calm. I directed
my question to one of the two sheepish campers. There was
no reply.

"Let's go take a look," I continued and beckoned the men to follow.

Their tent was a free-standing type that used no guy lines. One of the two gingerly lifted a side, exposing a tent-sized bed of spongy moss.

I couldn't believe what I was seeing. Holding back my anger I asked them if they had any idea how many hundreds of years it took for that bed of moss to cover the ridge. I also asked if they had any idea how many hundreds of campers had camped in this very spot and had not been tempted to cart pieces of the wilderness off to suit their comfort. And I also asked if they had any idea what this or any campsite would look like if the rest of the campers who used them abused them in the manner these fellows had. They had no answers. It was a roundabout way to give a minimum impact camping lecture.

They were embarrassed and I couldn't blame them. They had been caught red handed doing something that they knew was wrong, right from the outset. They had no excuses. Inside the tent, underneath the sleeping bags, lay comfortable foam pads. There had been no need to rip up the caribou moss.

Expressing their apologies eased my wrath and I suggested that maybe if we were careful we could put the moss back. I had no idea if it would ever again take hold but I figured the lesson would be worth our effort. I gave them a hand and we carried the large chunks to the ridge, putting them puzzle-like back on the naked pink granite. A few buckets of water helped to restore the plants' vigor. I'm pleased to report that by the end of the summer the moss had regained its grip and was apparently none the worse for its little trip.

While some of the damage done in the Canoe Country is perpetrated by just those you'd expect, thoughtless boors and vandals, much of it is done by otherwise well intentioned but uninformed, or perhaps just lazy, campers. In other words you and I. Yet no matter how nice the folks are that dirty a site, pollute the water or mar trees or plants, the results are the same as those acts who are done by vandals. Damage is done to this delicate resource.

The fact of the matter is that each and every year approximately 160,000 canoeists enter the Boundary Waters Canoe Area Wilderness and about one tenth that number visit the Quetico. That is a lot of folks. You and I are two of them. If you take each one of our actions and multiply it by that 175,000 visitors, you can quickly see that the effects on the Canoe Country are cumulative. If each of us cuts down a tree or builds a balsam bough or moss bed, then that is 175,000 felled trees or boughs or moss beds. That should be enough reason for us to be careful in our handling of this precious resource. But there is a greater reason.

Only you know why you chose to enter the wilderness. I go because of the sense of adventure, the calming powers of solitude, to do a little fishing and to shuck the coat of stifling city life. Each one of us must be aware of our reasons for going on a canoe trip before we enter, to be assured that our reasons are valid. The wilderness is not a place to go wild. It is not a place to practice survivalist techniques. The term "wilderness survival," the U.S. Forest Service likes to say, no longer means ones' ability to survive the wilderness but the ability of the wilderness to survive its visitors. And it is no joke.

In the end, we're talking about respect for the land. We're talking about a wilderness ethic where we do our best to leave no sign of our passing. If you need a challenge in the wilderness, accept this one. In this day and age we should be beyond trying to subdue what little wilderness is left and try to coexist. Think of it as being a guest in someone's home. For you truly are.

There are a number of things each of us can do to help preserve the wilderness of the Canoe Country. Our impact is greatest at two points: portages and campsites. The truth is, most of the Canoe Country goes unvisited but because we all use the same portages and campsites, our impact is most significant there. By using common sense and a little care, we can leave each place we touch unmarred.

There is no maid service in the Canoe Country. Rangers won't step into your site after you leave to clean it for the next campers. When Mary Jo and I were wilderness rangers we came upon one site where people actually piled up garbage and left a note for us. Seems they thought they were doing a good deed by putting the trash all in one spot. Wrong.

Many campsites on both sides of the border may not see a ranger once a year. If you leave trash, chances are it'll be there next year when you come back unless some thoughtful camper packed it out. And by that time, if the pile is still there, I guarantee it, will be much bigger. Nothing attracts garbage like garbage. If you leave a clean site, the next campers hopefully will try to leave it as clean. Leave garbage behind a bush and the next lazy camper will conclude that is the spot to deposit his. Each one of us is responsible for picking up any litter we find in the Canoe Country. Burn what you can and pack the rest out. After all, our food packs are empty on the return and our load light. A little trash will be easy to haul out. Your campsite is your responsibility. It can't be put any simpler than that.

It shouldn't have to be said but sadly it still needs to be repeated. Don't cut down trees or shrubs. While campers have been getting better over the years at not peeling bark or hacking down trees, the campsites get more denuded each season. The reason? The effects are becoming more noticeable over the years. It only takes one person to strip a birch or cut down a pine in a campsite each year and in ten years you have ten stripped birches or missing pines.

Late one night I heard a party arrive at the site below the cabin. Almost immediately I heard the thudding of an axe. When I finally had a chance to investigate we found a party trying to burn a green, only moments-before-alive, cedar tree. When I asked what they thought they were doing the leader mentioned that they wanted to cook some dinner. To my question of whether or not they had a camp stove, he rummaged around in his pack and produced a sophisticated mountaineering stove. He proceeded to sing its praises and told me just how many BTU's the little toy put out. He knew everything there was to know about that stove. He obviously didn't know anything about how to tell live trees from dead wood.

Next time you're in a campsite that has been picked clean of firewood, hop in your canoe and paddle down the shore a hundred yards. I guarantee you'll find more dead and easily obtainable firewood that you'd be able to burn in a year. A folding saw will be the only tool you'll ever need for making firewood on short trips.

Good minimum impact camping skills go beyond not destroying the obvious. Perhaps the greatest challenge most campers face is how to handle their own waste. At home you merely turn on the garbage disposal or flush the toilet. Soap is whisked down the drain and to a treatment center. Garbage is hauled to a landfill. We neither think about our refuse nor do we want to.

In the wilderness we must. A Canoe Country lake is neither a bathtub nor a kitchen sink. The bush immediately behind the tent is not a toilet. For our own sanitation and that of the next campers we must handle our waste. We simply have no right to pollute something as precious as the Canoe Country.

For some unknown reason we found that in many campsites people had made ah ... "pit stops" before they ever made it back to the Forest Service latrine. Believe me, the USFS doesn't put the latrines well back in the boonies to give the bears a crack at you. They are placed there because there is enough soil to dig a hole (a rarity in the Canoe Country), the distance from the water is sufficient to avoid pollution and it is screened for privacy.

No doubt some who didn't get back to the latrine found it difficult or scary to find in the dead of night. That's understandable. What isn't understandable is why they didn't go back in the daylight and bury their waste. Two minutes of your time will keep the campsite clean and avoid ruining someones' canoe trip when they stumble upon your surprise when gathering firewood.

The same is true for those emergency stops along portages. Avoid using the beginning and end of portage to handle your bodily functions. No chuckling folks, but the ends of some portages have become pretty unhealthy just a few yards back in the bushes. Go down the portage a distance and back into the woods a bit before answering that call of nature. We'll all appreciate it.

For goodness sake, please don't ever put anything down a latrine that doesn't belong there. Things that don't belong down a latrine are fuel cans, empty bug dope cans, leftover food, fish guts or broken fishing rods. These are all items that we commonly found in latrines during our duties as rangers. If I have to tell you what does belong down a latrine hole we're in big trouble. If anyone knew just how much work it was to dig a hole in the Canoe Country, indeed, to even find enough soil in which to dig a hole deep enough for a latrine, they'd never throw their garbage in one. Tossing trash down the hole only fills it in much sooner than need be. Food and fish guts only attracts flies and bears (neither are too delicate to let the other items found therein disturb their dining). Bears have been known to demolish a latrine to get at the garbage inside. Even without garbage down a latrine, some located at popular campsites need to be redug and moved every year. Just take my word for it. Digging latrines is no fun and the rangers really have more important things they could be doing.

If you're going into the Quetico please dig your own shallow pit latrine and insist that all your party members use it. Five minutes with a small shovel or garden trowel (for planting flowers) will give you a pit large enough for your entire party. Save any turf you cut away to put back on top after you've filled in the hole. If you do it right no one will ever be able to tell where you put your latrine. That's the way it should be.

There is an island campsite on the north end of Friday Bay of Crooked Lake. Mary Jo and I were down in this area doing some work when we were told about a dirty campsite by some passing canoeists. Seems someone had left some fish carcasses in camp. While this is not an uncommon problem, nothing could have prepared us for what we found. Over one hundred smallmouth bass, walleye and northern pike carcasses littered the rock shelf shoreline. Another hundred lay just under the water's surface off shore. We weren't just seeing the leavings of a careless camper but those of a group of first-class slobs. It was a long day cleaning up those fish and the rest of the trash we found in that site.

Fish remains are always a problem for campers. I mean, just what do you do with them? The USFS recommends you bury them well away from your campsite and the Quetico authorities suggest you put them out on a visible rock on the water's edge for scavengers to clean up. Notice that no one recommends you throw them in the lake. Nothing is more disgusting than stooping to scoop up a bucket full of lake water only to have the partially decayed remains of a walleye staring back up at you. My own method is to put the fish remains out for the gulls. If they don't clean them (which usually happens while you're still eating the fillets), then I take them well back into the woods and bury them. Most of the time I won't have to.

Don't bury them near camp. Some busy campsites have a distinctly fishy odor because many campers don't want to get out of sight of their tent before burying the fish. It isn't many days before they get ripe smelling and start to attract insects and bears. Burying fish near camp is just like posting an invitation for bears.

There is no good reason for washing yourself or your dishes in the lakes and streams. Even biodegradable soap is pollution. It doesn't just disappear. Imagine the 160,000 BWCAW visitors taking at least one complete bath each year in a lake. That's a lot of soap and shampoo. And you're drinking it.

Doing your dishes in the largest pot of your cook kit is the easiest means and allows you to do it with hot water instead of cold lake water. Take them back in the woods a short distance and scrub and rinse them back there. The microbes in the topsoil will quickly break down both any food bits or soap. If you have leftover food, burn it in a hot fire to avoid attracting bears. Better yet, have a teenager with you. There won't be any leftovers.

Taking a bath or washing your hair is no different. We usually jump in for a swim and then go back up on shore, well away from the water, before lathering up. Whoever isn't bathing mans the bucket brigade and passes up the rinse water. After knocking off as much soap as possible back in the bushes, we go for another swim. It is a simple procedure and we have the pride in knowing that we've done our best to avoid polluting the lake.

Even though the BWCAW allows you to travel in groups of ten, and the Quetico in groups of nine, concerned campers will travel in smaller groups if possible. Small groups can pack lighter, travel faster, explore more country and see more wildlife. Both you and the wilderness will benefit if you travel in small groups.

Occasionally we ran into large groups, really large groups, like the outing group from a university that had twenty-one people. When I asked for their permit the group leaders smiled and produced three. They were legal, or so they thought, since each permit allowed up to ten. They didn't smile quite as much when I turned the permit over and read to them rule #2 which states that not only is party size limited to ten, you can't be in groups of more than ten at any time or place in the BWCAW. This means that no matter how many permits you have, you can't travel or camp together if you number more than ten. Period. Rules for the Quetico are similar.

Finally, if you're in the BWCAW, camp only in designated campsites (firegrate and latrine). Those who camp in non-designated sites only invite others to do so because it begins to look like a campsite. The USFS has located present sites according to a number of criteria such as privacy and the ability to place a firegrate in a safe place and a non-polluting latrine. Start looking for a campsite in the early afternoon and rarely will you be unable to find one. If you reach your destination and find all sites occupied, push on. A permit is not a reservation for a particular campsite on a particular lake. The nature of wilderness travel is that sometimes you must exert yourself beyond what you intended. You accepted that challenge when you entered the Canoe Country. It will be an unusual case if another mile won't put you near an empty site. Be familiar with your map and compass and get off the main travel routes into back bays. You'll find the campsites there less likely to be occupied and generally cleaner and less worn. They are always more private.

For those who don't believe these rules make sense the two governments managing the Canoe Country do make it a point to send out law enforcement people. Few things will dampen a visit faster than a $50 to $500 fine, or a trip before a judge. It should never have to come to that.

Fortunately for all of us, most campers do a good job at cleaning up after themselves. Many take home more than their own trash in an effort to preserve the character of the wilderness or go out of their way to be quiet and unobtrusive to other campers. Mary Jo and I found that even those who were doing things improperly were almost always doing them only because they thought it did no harm or they knew no other way. This is where each of us can play a big role. If you are in a group that is practicing poor or outmoded camping techniques, point out the proper way. Don't back down. It is your wilderness you're saving. Ultimately it is our responsibility to safeguard the Canoe Country, to educate other members of our group and to teach respect.

Only through respect can we come to deal with the wilderness on its own terms, gain a feel for its purity, put our finger on its pulse and find our own niche in its schemes. Too long have we been the subduer. Our challenge now is not to subdue nature but to discover how we can live within its terms. This is the hope of the entire planet. Learning to do so on your next canoe trip might just be the place to begin your lessons.

Epilogue

Going Alone – a Trip to Canoe Country

EINO MAKI'S back hurt. He put each foot down carefully, watching where they were placed, mindful of the rocks and roots. The old canoe on his shoulders felt heavier than he ever could remember, though he knew its weight hadn't really changed. Despite the weight, it felt good to have it on his shoulders once more.

The portage had seemed longer, the hills steeper, the trail rougher. He knew too that this was only in his mind, that it was the years that made it seem so and that the young bucks could still fly across this portage. He had.

The trail climbed out of the dark evergreen forest and into a little clearing, a small knob of ancient green stone that is the bone of this part of the canoe country. At the top of the hill stood two enormous pines, towering whites that had somehow been spared when this land had been logged a half century ago. Between the pines a cross member of spruce had been lashed some ten feet above the ground. Eino pushed the bow of the canoe up onto this rest with a grunt and stepped from beneath it, knocking his battered old fedora from his head. He slipped the patched Duluth pack from his shoulders and swung it to the ground, leaning it up against a boulder. Although he was traveling lightly, much lighter than was usual on his canoe trips, the pack and canoe had built up a searing pain between his shoulder blades.

Eino stepped aside and arched his back with his elbows pointing to the rear, pushing them toward each other as if to touch, forcing the kinks from his muscles. Hat still off, he dug a bandana from the back pocket of his wool trousers and wiped his brow.

From the top of this knob was a view of the lake. As it always had, it shone a brilliant blue through the forest. But at this time of year, autumn, when much of the undergrowth was down, Eino thought it particularly brilliant. He could make out, across the lake, the tattered red flag of a mountain maple, solitary in its splendor amidst the golden aspens. Walking a few yards to the highest point of the little outcrop, the lichens crunching under his boots, he sunk to the ground. The rock beneath him was cool despite the heat of the summer which had recently ended. Though it was sunny this day, the air was crisp and the nights had been colder. The sun on his woolen clothing was warm. It felt good. Looking through the trees to the lake he felt relieved that he was almost there. He had often stopped at this point for the view on previous trips. This time it was for the rest as well. It hadn't always been so.

Eino had come a long way this day. Seven portages was a good day for anyone and he took some small pride in the fact he had accomplished this task as old and as sick as he was. No one would believe he could have travelled so far. He was sure they wouldn't look for him here. Not soon, anyway.

Not that he didn't feel bad that it had to be this way. But his wife and bow paddler of forty years was gone now and there was no one else that really understood. Not his kids. To them he was an old romantic fool. He hoped that someday they might understand.

No, he had to go alone, just as he had as a young man so many years ago. He knew the first time he ever saw this country that it would be the place not only for his youth, but for his old age. Yes, he had thought of this trip even then. What he would do when the time came. At that time it had even seemed a bit romantic and foolish to him. Now it seemed right.

"Dad," his daughter had said, "really, I don't know why you're being so difficult. I wish you wouldn't be so stubborn. The doctors say you can lick this. You'll be able to make it. Why, you'll just have to take it easy, that's all. No more of your silly running around in the woods. You need plenty of rest. And you'll have to go in for treatments a few times a week. We'll sell your place and you can move into town. I've already been over to Pleasant Acres. It looks nice. Lots of friendly people your age. You'll like it there."

Bullshit. Pure, unadulterated bullshit, that's what it is. I'll be damned if I'll live with a bunch of bed wetting, can't feed themselves zombies. And they can take their "treatment" and shove it. No one ever said anything about licking this thing to me. No sir. You'll be able to go on quite a bit longer, that's what they said. Told me I'd have to quit exerting myself, come in for treatments, take that damn poison they call medicine and stay in bed. That is what they told me. Smartass kid doctors. Who the hell wants to "go on quite a bit longer?"

Eino coughed and it felt like his lungs were going to come out of his mouth. He spat.

Well, there was no time to worry about all this. He'd left a note on the kitchen table at home. He wouldn't look backward now. He had to make camp before it grew much later. There was still a fair distance to go.

Eino shouldered the pack and got under the canoe, straining to lift it from the rest. He swung the bow around and pointed it down the portage. It was all downhill from here and he thought he'd better be careful if he didn't want to go ass over tea kettle down the rocky trail.

The blue of the lake grew larger through the trees. Excited as he always had been by that sight, Eino pushed himself to the water's edge.

"Never was a very good put-in spot," he said to no one as he surveyed the rocky shore for a place to set down the canoe.

Wading out to his boot tops he rolled the aged craft gently onto the water. Sliding the Duluth pack from his shoulders he put it on the canoe floor behind the bow thwart and at the same time freed a paddle from where it had been wedged in the bow. Pulling his jacket from under the lash-down straps of the pack, he folded it double and laid it on the floor in front of the stern thwart. Eino eased himself into the canoe, one hand on each gunwale, shaking the water from his boots. He knelt upon the jacket, his back against the thwart. Picking up the paddle he gave two swift, shallow strokes and floated out from under the cedars.

The wind was blowing soft but steadily toward the point he had planned on camping upon. Eino let the wind do most of the work, thankful for the rest. He sat back on his crossed ankles, paddling infrequently, watching the forested shore drift by. He wondered if the lake trout were biting. He also studied the empty bow seat. Eino looked away, his eyes falling on the well worn cedar of the Chestnut canoe's ribs and planks. Though aged, they were sound, whole. No rot had crept into their fibers.

Eino recalled when he purchased the canoe. "Why, this canoe will outlast you!" the salesman had said. Sonafabitchin' prophet.

In the north country autumn nights come early and Eino realized he had much to do before dark. He stirred himself from his recollections and picked up the pace of his paddling, feeling the icy water splash on his lower hand every few strokes. The point took form on the horizon, rising from its watery island mirage to become connected to the mainland. The little open area beneath the tall pines at the very tip of the point grew more defined and looked inviting.

This had been his very favorite campsite in all of the canoe country. It had a perfect flat spot for the tent with, miraculously in this thin skinned land, enough soil for firm tent pegs. The

189

point stuck far out into the lake and most always had a breeze, which Eino liked for better fire draft and bug relief. A large sloping rock shelf that lay under the whole of the point tipped into the water at the point's terminus. There was even a perfect berth into which a canoe could be paddled, carved out of the rock. The berth was deep enough that the canoe did not scrape yet sloped to one side, making climbing in and out of the canoe simple. Just up the slope from this slot was a thick bed of caribou moss that made an ideal spot for rolling over the canoe without damaging the wooden decks or gunwales. And off the north side of the point ran a reef which always had lake trout cruising about it.

Eino nudged the bow of the canoe into its berth and creakily climbed ashore. He carried the pack and paddle up the slope to the campsite and propped both against the bole of a giant pine. Walking back down to the canoe and grabbing it amidship, he carried it a little way up the smooth rock slope.

Though he hadn't been there in years, Eino found the campsite had not changed much from his last visit. A large pine branch fallen across the tent pad proved that he was the first camper here in some time. He dragged the wood down to the fire ring. It was dry and resinous and would be all the firewood he would need for dinner.

Dinner! It surprised him that eating was on his mind. All the time he had been sick this past year, food was of little interest to him. He had shrunk to the weight of his fit twenties. But the exercise of the day had made even a sick man hungry and he thought of perhaps catching a lake trout for dinner. First, though, he rummaged around in his pack and removed what he needed.

With the tent up, Eino turned to the firewood. He broke as much of the branch as he could into foot long pieces by leaning it against a log and stomping on it. The few arm thickness chunks at the branch's base fell quickly to his folding saw. He piled it all up neatly along side the fire ring and dug into his pockets for the strips of birchbark he had stuffed there, strips that he had picked up along the portages shed by the birches. Gathering a few twigs for tinder was easy and he was shortly set for the evening.

Eino was amazed at how good he was feeling. Why, he hadn't felt this good, though tired, in many a long month. Maybe, he thought, maybe I should have listened to those doctors. Maybe I could have licked this thing.

"Either way," he said aloud, "either way I'm damn hungry. Wonder if there's a laker or two still off this point?"

Eino went down to the canoe once again and unlashed his old rod from the slotted gunwales. Setting the rod aside he picked up the canoe and carried it on his hip up to the caribou moss and set it down. "It'll be fine here," he said, rolling it over.

Back at the pack he retrieved a small box that contained a few odds and ends of fishing tackle. He also pulled out a small plastic bag which held the big salted shiner minnows he had picked up at the bait shop on his drive to the trail head. Eino threaded a shiner on his hook, pinched on a few sinkers a couple of feet up the line and walked to the water's edge at the tip of the point. With a heave he flipped the rig out into the lake. Eino put the reel on free spool and stuck the rod's butt in a crevice of the shelf rock. Two bread loaf sized rocks, one each in front and behind the rod handle, would hold the works in place.

All of this activity, and the day's hard work, was beginning to wear on Eino. Getting his sleeping bag he carried it down to the shelf rock near the rod, spreading it flat in the late afternoon sun. He sat down slowly on the bag. Taking out a hip flask, Eino poured a couple of fingers of brandy into a battered camp cup and drew a sip.

"S'pose the damn doctors wouldn't much like this," he chuckled.

He looked down at the tarnished silver flask. It had been an anniversary present from his wife. God, how he had missed her these last years! How he missed her now! Gazing out over the darkening waters of the lake he thought of her and downed his drink in a silent toast. Eino recalled the first time they had camped on this point together when he was young and strong and she was so beautiful. How, on a warm and sunny day they had spread out their sleeping bags after lunch on this very same rock. He remembered her warm touch and how they had made love in the open air and had finally drifted off to sleep. What a sight they would have been if someone had come along! Eino smiled at that thought and laid back on the bag lost in his youth, dreaming of her. He closed his eyes after one last glance at the tip of his fishing rod.

At first all was black. Then he could make out a red glow, as though he could see the blood in his eyelids backed by the setting sun. Out of the glow stepped his young wife walking gracefully toward him, arms outstretched.

In the clear waters of the lake a trout swam up to the shiner minnow. It nosed around the bait cautiously and bumped the minnow with the side of its body. Turning around the fish engulfed the shiner in one quick motion and swam swiftly off. Feeling the sting of the hook it made a rapid run many yards along the top of the reef. In and out of the boulders the trout swam, trying to free itself of the trailing line. Up on shore the rod tip bucked, the reel whined and the line unraveled. But there was no one there to stop it. Reaching the end, it parted.

Addendum

A jewel of rare value, the Quetico-Superior wilderness is the finest canoe country in the world. No other place combines such a vast number of sparkling lakes connected by wild creeks, rivers or short portages. Given the inclination, a visitor to this country could travel for months and never see the same place twice, each new vista more beautiful than the last. The Boundary Waters and Quetico are as distinctive and worthy of protection as is the Grand Canyon, the Florida Everglades or any other natural, and what some would consider more "exotic," wonder of the world.

With the great pleasure you will be enjoying in exploring and fishing this wilderness comes the very real responsibility to treat the country with respect. This is not an option. No one has the right to defile this boreal wonder. It does not exist solely for human pleasure or use. We can fit in where we may, enjoy the splendor as we might but in the end, we must pass through without leaving any sign.

Precisely because visiting the Canoe Country can be such a glorious experience, it has been besieged by canoeing and fishing enthusiasts. To try to retain some semblance of wilderness, the two agencies that manage this international ecosystem have placed limits on the number of people that may enter on any given day or at any single place, restrict party size and require that all visitors carry a permit. Visitors are also required to leave canned or bottled foods and drinks at home and, in the BWCAW, to camp only in designated campsites. The regulations governing the BWCAW and Quetico are very similar and you are required to become familiar with them. Ignorance is no excuse; the rules come with your permit and you are duty bound to obey them. If you do not, the wilderness and other visitors suffer and you may face the very real prospect of a citation and fine.

Separate permits are needed for the BWCAW and Quetico. They are easy to obtain and can be reserved in advance. While we will cover the "how-to" in procuring your permit, such procedures change from time to time and the ultimate source for this information will be either the U.S. Forest Service or Quetico Provincial Park officials. Check with them if you have any doubts.

A BWCAW permit allows a party of up to nine in four watercraft to enter the area on a specific day and at one location only. The date and location is up to you, depending, of course, on whether quotas are full. Boundary Waters permits can be reserved by phone beginning February 1 of each year. To reserve a BWCAW permit, call 1-800-745-3399. You must inform them at this time of your date and point of entry. Your permit will then be reserved, for a $5.00 fee chargeable to VISA or MasterCard, and held for your arrival. Permits must be picked up in person by the group leader or designated alternate (ID required) at any Superior National Forest office during the 24-hour period before your departure. During the busy season, most offices have extended hours; check for the exact schedule.

Of course, you don't need to reserve your BWCAW permit and you may simply walk into one of the offices and apply for one. On all but the busiest of holiday weekends, a permit will be available for some entry point but, if you have your heart set on a particular route, you'd really be wise to take advantage of the reservation system. Those using motors to enter the BWCAW on routes where they are allowed need a special day use, motor permit, which are limited in number, and can be reserved at the toll free number. Beginning October 1, 1995, all other day use visitors to the BWCAW will also need a day use permit. Since these are unlimited in number, no reservation need be made.

The permit allows you to enter only on that day and at that entry point, nothing else. You are free to travel wherever the wanderlust takes you but you must camp at only a designated

USFS campsite. Permits do not guarantee a campsite at the lake you had hoped to fish and on busy weekends you may just find that all sites are full. You must move on then to another lake so be prepared and allow yourself extra time in the case of that event.

BWCAW campsites are marked on Fisher and McKenzie maps and, for the most part, the maps are very accurate. Just because there is a red dot on the map, however, doesn't mean you may camp there. From time to time the USFS closes overused campsites and older maps may not reflect those changes. If where you stop does not have both a permanent steel firegrate in place and a wooden or fiberglass wilderness latrine, you are not allowed to camp there. Move on. By camping illegally you invite arrest and damage the resource.

You may also reserve permits for Quetico Provincial Park if your canoe trip falls between the third Friday in May and the end of the Labor Day weekend. If you enter the Quetico before that date in May you need do nothing but check through customs (if you are driving) or call Canadian customs if you are paddling it from the BWCAW. After Labor Day weekend, and until the Canadian Thanksgiving holiday (early October), you can self register and pay your fees at any of the entry points.

To reserve a Quetico permit you may either write to the Ministry of Natural Resources, 108 Saturn Avenue, Atikoken, Ontario, Canada, POT 1C0 or call them at (807) 597-2735. There is a $6.00 (Canadian funds) service charge for the reservation. When phoning in you will be asked for the number of your VISA or MasterCard, but the credit card will not be charged until you actually pick up the permit when you depart. Permits must be picked up by the group leader you specified on the phone, or an alternate (also given over the phone) at the entry point you specified on the date reserved. Unlike the BWCAW, there is an overnight camping fee for Quetico users. For each party member 18 or older you will be charged $4.25 (Canadian) per night. Younger visitors, ages 12 through 17, get by for $2.25 per night. If you cancel your trip to the Quetico, and have reserved a permit, you must let them know. If you fail to cancel before at least one day prior to your departure date, and you do not show up to pick up your permit, the park authorities will charge your credit card with the reservation fee and one night's camping fee for each person in your party.

Ontario fishing licenses are available at all the entry point ranger stations and may also be charged to your credit card, or they may be picked up at many of the outfitters in the Aitikoken area if you are driving to the north side of the park.

All Quetico visitors must check in and obtain a permit at one of the six ranger stations. These stations, scattered around the park's periphery, are Beaverhouse Lake, French Lake, Nym Lake, Lac La Croix, Prairie Portage on Basswood Lake and Cache Bay on Saganaga Lake. They are operated from mid-May to mid-September.

Remember, you must also clear Canadian Customs before entering Quetico. If you drive to the northern entry points you will clear customs at the border. Those paddling into the park must first check in at either Saganaga, Basswood or Sandpoint Customs Office. Your permit confirmation comes with a packet of information that will give you further details about all of these procedures.

Quetico Park allows many fewer people to enter than does the BWCAW, even though the two areas are of equal size. Consequently, although solitude is easier to find in the Quetico, reserving a permit for your long-planned trip is very important. The busiest entry points, and the ones that fill up first, are those serviced by the Prairie Portage ranger station on Basswood Lake.

You may have up to nine persons in your party on one Quetico permit and when in the park, are free to travel or camp wherever you wish. Since there are no designated campsites, there are also no firegrates or latrines. Locate your fire on a rock shelf, or other safe mineral soil, near the water's edge. And for pete's sake, dig a small latrine hole well back in the woods, away from the water, and insist that all members of your party use it! When you leave, fill in the latrine and cover it with natural duff so you'll leave the area pleasant for the next party. The lack of such common sense sanitation is Quetico's worst problem.

You may not bring any live baitfish into Quetico Provincial Park, nor are firearms or fireworks allowed.

While your BWCAW permit allows up to nine people in four watercraft, you cannot circumvent those restrictions by getting additional permits for a larger party and then traveling together. The maximum party size must be obeyed at all times, even on the water. In other words, if you have twenty people that want to go on a trip, you may not camp or travel with each other in groups larger than allowed no matter how many permits you obtain.

Both the BWCAW and Quetico have a bottle and can ban for foodstuffs. Bug spray, fuel or toiletries are allowed in such containers though. Everyone is required to have a personal flotation device. Check with the Minnesota DNR or Ontario MNR for current fishing license requirements and fees.

Outboard motors, including electric ones, are banned throughout the Quetico, except in a limited area to members of the Lac La Croix Ojibway Indian band and in most of the BWCAW. There are some lakes in the BWCAW on which motors are allowed and on most of these there are horsepower restrictions. The majority of the BWCAW,however, is off-limits to motorized or mechanized travel. If you plan on using a motor, check with the USFS for details on the restrictions and permits needed.

Burn all your burnable trash and pack out the rest. Obtain and carry both good maps and a compass. A first-rate first-aid kit is a must and be sure you know how to use it. Be considerate of others and keep your noise level down. Sound carries great distances in this country and no one paddled their butt off to listen to you. Leave your damn radio at home.

If you've never before camped or canoed, you would be best off employing the services of one of the region's excellent outfitters. You may obtain information about them by writing to area Chambers of Commerce, listed at the end of this chapter.

Finally, now is the time to question whether you really want a wilderness canoe trip. This is rugged country and requires that you put out effort in reaching it and in preserving it. Although photos of this country rarely show it in anything but the most pleasant weather, it does, believe me, rain and storm. Wind can turn the lakes into tossing seas, pinning you for hours or days. Biting insects can be more than just bothersome, they can drive you absolutely insane. Portages are not always smooth or dry; some will be up to your knees in muck. There are no signs to direct you, nor are there picnic tables. In other words, a visit to this country is not always easy. If you must have a beer while you're fishing, like loud sing-a-longs in the evening, or feel all these aforementioned restrictions are too imposing, fine. Go somewhere else. The Canoe Country needs only conscientious visitors and those willing to put up with its worst to experience its best. It is not for everyone.

The Canoe Country is magnificent for those who are open to it. For every difficulty experienced while on a trip, there is at least one reward. Deep within its stony bosom beats the heart of our very beginnings; the rhythm of the wilderness. Wonder and magic is everywhere for those whose senses have not been dulled excessively by our modern life.

To those who love the wilderness, who are not afraid of muck and sweat, who do not fear the wildlife or wild weather, who can tolerate the insects and brave long portages, the Canoe Country will be good to you. Be good to it. If, on your travels, you see a man and a woman in a red wood and canvas canoe, most likely with a blockheaded labrador retriever riding in it like a queen, paddle over quietly. I'd like to meet you. And I usually know where the fish are biting.

Have a damn fine trip.

USFS District Offices
(Visitor permits, BWCAW info)

LaCroix Ranger District
Box 1085
Cook, MN 55723
(218) 666-5151

Tofte Ranger District
Tote, MN 55615
(218) 663-7981

Kawishiwi Ranger District
118 S. 4th Ave. E.
Ely, MN 55731
(218) 365-6185

Gunflint Ranger District
Box 308
Grand Marais, MN 55604
(218) 387-1750

BWCAW Information
Superior National Forest
P.O. Box 338
Duluth, MN 55801
(218) 720-5324 (info only)
1-800-745-3399 (reservations)

MN Department of Natural Resources
(Licensing info, etc.)

MN Department of Natural Resources
Box 40, Lafayette Road
St. Paul, MN 55155
(toll-free) 1-800-766-6000

Quetico Provincial Park
(Permit or fishing license information)

Ontario Ministry of Natural Resources
108 Saturn Avenue
Atikoken, Ontario
Canada   POT 1C0
(807) 587-6971

ADDENDUM

Quetico Permit Reservations
(807) 597-2735

(Info on specific lakes, fish in area)

MN DNR Fisheries Headquarters
P.O. Box 146
Grand Marais, MN 55604
(218) 387-2535

MN DNR Fisheries Headquarters
S.R. # 2, Box 3710
Ely, MN 55731
(218) 365-3230

MN DNR Fisheries Headquarters
P.O. Box 546
Finland, MN 55603
(218) 353-7591

MN DNR Fisheries Headquarters
Rt. 8, Box 8
International Falls, MN 56649
(218) 286-5434

Tourist Information
(Outfitters, Lodges, Campgrounds, Motels)

Cook Chamber of Commerce
Cook, MN 55723
(218) 666-5375

Atikoken Chamber of Commerce
P.O. Box 997
Atikoken, Ontario
Canada   POT 1C0

Ely Chamber of Commerce
1600 F. Sheridan St.
Ely, MN 55731
(218) 365-6123

Tip of the Arrowhead Assoc.
15 N. Broadway
Grand Marais, MN 55604
(218) 387-2524

Lutsen-Tofte Tourism Assoc.
Box 115
Lutsen, MN 55612
(218) 663-7804